W9-BTJ-167

Sabrine d'Aubergine

Christmas at last!

Holiday recipes and stories from Italy

All grown-ups were children once.
(But only a few of them remember it).

The Little Prince, Antoine de Saint-Exupéry

To Claudia,
who gazes at the Christmas tree enchanted.
I hope she'll never forget having been a child.

Sabrine d'Aubergine

Christmas at last!

Holiday recipes and stories from Italy

Guido Tommasi Editore

Contents

Introduction

Come December, the house begins to dance to an unmistakeable and joyous rhythm. There is a festive frenzy, an atmosphere of expectation… And while decorations and memories come out of boxes, and the tree lights up, and the gift list gets shorter – as parcels pop up here and there – even the most thick-skinned ones decide the moment has come to lay down their armour and be children again: and they surrender to Christmas. The Christmas spirit is, by its intimate nature, somewhat regressive. Without even realising it, we find ourselves believing in Father Christmas, gazing at a hot chocolate without any dietary worries, digging out old Christmas films and vintage songs, and even certain reindeer knitted jumpers from elderly aunts otherwise destined to lie among mothballs and family relics. But if you are anything like me, and you're among those who can't wait to surrender and welcome Santa with open arms – because a tad of regression is just what's needed, once a year, to balance out eleven months of being an adult – this book will give you something to really get your teeth into. This is the story of a little kitchen – a real kitchen, just like your own – that comes alive with edible adventures during the run up to Christmas. And if ingredients and characters intertwine as well as stories and recipes, it's because that's how life really works… There's no hint of a professional chef around these parts! Cooking is a way of being together and loving each other, so the aim is not "what to eat at Christmas", but rather "how to have fun in the kitchen, while making the most of the relaxed pace of Christmas". This is how delicious gifts end up under the Christmas tree: biscuits, syrups, pâtés, nougat and other crunchy stuff, jars of chutney and jellies, pot-pourri… There are recipes that will also, with a few added extras, bring improvised snacks between friends to life, or enhance traditional family dinners.

We come together in the kitchen to share memories, have a little tipple, slow-cook some beef stew in mulled wine, or get all hands on deck to knead delicious brioches for a guilt-free breakfast or *merenda*.

And while wreaths – of sweet buns, profiteroles, meringues or orange stars – entwine, and spice scents merrily dance in the air, the house gets ready for the celebration that thrills old and young alike: clouds of flour rise and snowflakes fall, but made out of sugar… In this book you'll find recipes that anyone can make, even those who would never have thought they had culinary talents: you risk starting to read a story and then find your fingers stuck into a silky dough that smells of butter! You have been warned… Many of the recipes are the edible equivalent of a comfy, much-loved armchair in a peaceful corner of the house, because that spent at the stove is always a light-hearted time, and it doesn't matter if your cake comes out a bit lopsided: at Christmas everyone is kind, no-one will say a word if you've made it with love!

And now I think I've told you everything, at least all what I can fit into one page: all that remains is for me to wish you happy reading and happy cooking! And a merry, sparkling Christmas, full of dreams waiting to come true. Surrender yourself to its magic. And wherever you are and whomever you're with – under the starry skies of this small crazy world – do whatever you can to be happy. Buon Natale!

Sabine

A little bakery
for celebration days

Almond and fig brioches

TIME: 3½-4 HOURS
(2 BATCHES)

MAKES 12 BRIOCHES

FOR THE DOUGH
350 g/12 oz bread flour
150 g/2 oz all-purpose flour
A pinch of salt
150 ml/5 fl oz milk
80 g/just over 3 oz caster sugar
25 g/1 oz compressed fresh yeast
3 large eggs
80 g/just over 3 oz soft butter
(plus a knob to grease the bowl)

FOR THE FILLING
50 g/2 oz dried figs
30 g/just over 1 oz butter
40-50 g/1½-2 oz mandorlina
(see note)

FOR THE FINISHING
2 tablespoons caster sugar dissolved
in 1 tablespoon water

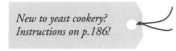

New to yeast cookery?
Instructions on p.186!

1. Put the flour and salt into a large bowl and mix with a whisk (this is to lighten them up, having been so compacted in their packaging…). Gently warm the milk.

2. Put 1 tablespoon of sugar, taken from the total, into a bowl and cream with the yeast, i.e. crumble together only the yeast and sugar, as if you are working with plasticine. Add the milk, mix with your fingers to dissolve the yeast, then add about a third of the flour mixture. Whisk to break any lumps: the mixture should have the soft consistency of a batter or a hot béchamel sauce. Seal with cling film and leave to rest for 20 minutes in a warm place.

3. In the meantime, separate the eggs and whip the whites until stiff with three quarters of the sugar (if you whisk by hand, add the sugar gradually: it's less tiring).

4. Make a well in the flour and pour the yeast in slowly, without mixing; cover with the whipped whites and then a layer of flour taken from the edges, without breaking the well. Leave to rest for 15 minutes.

5. Add the yolks, beaten with the remaining sugar, and the soft butter. Mix with a spoon until it becomes hard to stir, then use your hands (you need one to mix and the other to hold the bowl firmly). Pinch part of the dough from the edge, stretch it outwards, then fold it back into the centre. Turn the bowl a few degrees, pinch another part of the dough and repeat the movement. Continue with these stretches and folds for about 5 minutes, until the ingredients are evenly mixed and the dough comes away from the sides of the bowl.

6. Then transfer your dough onto the worktop, and work it with the "grab-beat-fold" technique (more details on p. 186): grab it with one hand, beat it on the worktop holding it in your hand and fold it onto itself, give it a quarter turn and start again. After 200 folds (count them, it's relaxing), that is about 10 minutes, the dough will be smooth and no longer sticky.

7. Place the dough back into the clean and freshly buttered bowl, seal with cling film, and leave to rise in a warm place until doubled in volume (about an hour and a half).

In the meantime, soak the figs in a bowl of warm water.

8. When the dough is almost ready, preheat the oven to 220°C/430°F and line a baking tray with parchment paper. Get everything you need for the filling ready: melt the butter, squeeze the water out of the figs and chop them into small pieces.

9. Gently deflate the dough and flatten it out with your hands into a 30 x 50 cm/ 12" x 19 ½" rectangle: be nice and give it time to spread out without squashing it brutally. Brush with melted butter (leave a spoonful aside for the finishing), and spread the *mandorlina* and dried figs on one half of the rectangle. Fold the other half over the filling and gently press down, to allow the two halves to stick together (they may rebel, but you just carry on).
Cut the rectangle (which will now be 25 x 30 cm/10" x 12") into 12 strips lengthwise. Use a sharp knife or a round pizza-cutter (no a serrated edges!): the figs will try to escape, and the *mandorlina* will attempt to follow, but don't panic! Behave as if

recipes

nothing is happening: you can distribute anything that is left on the worktop among the brioches... Twist each strip into a spiral (as if it is a length of string), and tie a knot: don't worry if they don't look so graceful, just round them off a little as if they were meatballs, and place them on the tray, leaving some space between each one (you need to plan for two batches: cover the second batch with clingfilm, and leave to wait on the worktop).

10. Leave the brioches to rise for 15-20 minutes in a large, inflated, well-secured plastic bag, brush them with the remaining butter and pop them in the oven for about 15 minutes. After the first ten minutes, remove the tray from the oven, quickly brush over the final glaze and put it back to finish cooking: they should be little more than golden to remain soft inside. Place them on a cooling rack, then put the remaining 6 in the oven (they will have already risen, so you only need to brush them with butter).

❄ *Mandorlina: this is what I call a mixture of toasted mandorle (almonds) and cane sugar in a ratio of 4 to 5 (so 40g/ just over 1 oz almonds for every 50g/2oz sugar), finely chopped in a blender. You can prepare it in advance: with this quantity you will get double the amount you need for this recipe, but with less you won't manage it. Keep the excess in a glass jar and use it to garnish biscuits, brioches and chocolate truffles.*

❄ *Remove the eggs and butter from the fridge before you start. The butter needs to be soft ("beurre pommade", as the French call it) to melt slowly in the warmth of the dough. And, as far as eggs are concerned, the whites become friends with sugar more easily when they are at room temperature. After all, a meeting between two chilled to the bone people could never lead to explosive passion (and a meringue is most definitely the result of explosive passion, I can assure you...).*

❄ *Every oven has its own timing habits, so cooking times should be taken "cum grano salis"... even if you are baking something sweet! A clock is important – the only one in my house is in the kitchen – but in some cases eyes work better than clocks. So, this is not the time to declutter your wardrobe, start working in the garden, or call your friend betrayed by her husband: stay nearby and switch on the light! The oven light...*

recipes

A brioche wreath

Time: 3½-4 hours

For the dough
350 g/12 oz bread flour
A pinch of salt
150 ml/5 fl oz milk
50 ml/just over 1 oz kefir
60 g/just over 2 oz caster sugar
12 g/½ oz compressed fresh yeast
40 g/just under 2 oz butter (plus a
    knob to grease the bowl)
2 large egg yolks

For the filling
100 g/4 oz dark chocolate
    (70% cocoa)
100 g/4 oz dried pitted prunes (very
    soft)

For the finishing
2 tablespoons caster sugar dissolved
    in 1 tablespoon water

New to yeast cookery?
Instructions on p.186!

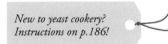 *If the prunes aren't very soft it will be impossible to blend them without adding any liquid. Much better to act on prevention: soak them in a little warm water before blending, and then squeeze them out before using.*

1. In a large bowl, whisk together the flours and salt and make a well in the centre. Weigh the sugar and leave it on the scales.

2. Gently warm the milk; add the kefir, 1 tablespoon sugar and 1 heaped tablespoon flour (taken from the respective total), and the crumbled yeast. Mix well until the yeast is dissolved and leave to rest in a warm place for about 15 minutes: it should double in volume. In the meantime, beat the yolks gently with the melted butter (allow to cool before using). Add the rest of the sugar to the flour.

3. Pour the yeast and the butter and yolk mixture into the bowl with the flour. Mix with a spoon until it becomes hard to stir, then use your hands: pinch a part of the dough from the edge, stretch it outwards, then fold it back into the center. Turn the bowl a few degrees, pinch another part of the dough and repeat the movement. Continue with these stretches and folds for a few minutes, until the ingredients are evenly mixed.

4. Transfer your dough onto the worktop, leave under the upturned bowl for 5 minutes, then knead with the "snakes & snails" technique (see p. 186), stretching and rolling the dough for 10-12 times (about 10 minutes). It shouldn't be as sticky now, and it'll become even less sticky as you go along. Anyway, don't be tempted to add more flour at this stage: all you need is a little butter on your hands and worktop, to keep it under control.

5. Place the dough back in a clean bowl greased with butter, seal with cling film and allow to rise until doubled in volume (it will take between 1 hour and an hour and a half).

6. When the dough is almost ready, prepare the filling. Cut the prunes into small pieces and reduce them to a pulp with the hand blender: it won't be easy because the mixture is very dry, but try every technique you can to avoid adding liquid (which would make your brioche too dampish).
Melt the chocolate and add it to the prunes (the mixture should now be more fluid, but the effect will only last until the chocolate dries).

7. Transfer the dough onto the worktop (no extra flour!) and begin to spread it out with your fingers. Allow time for it to realise that it needs to form a rectangle, and comply with its natural inclination to draw back: forceful methods don't work. Use a rolling pin to help you (not as a club!) only at the end: you need a rectangle about 30 x 40 cm/12" x 19.5" in size. Spread the filling leaving a 3 cm/just over 1" edge on the long side nearest to you. It's very thick, it will be quite difficult to spread, so make small piles and use your fingers to distribute it as evenly as you can. Roll the dough starting with the long side opposite you; moisten the edge with water before closing the roll, which should be tight, and seal it by pinching with your fingers.

8. Cut the roll lengthwise with a sharp knife (seam side down), until you reach 2 cm/ just under 1" from the end. Weave the two halves passing one on top of another, and keeping the cut side high. Then form a circle, seal the outer edges, and... stand back and admire it! Your wreath will give you a smile!

9. Place the wreath on a baking tray lined with parchment paper, and allow to rise for half an hour in a large, inflated well secured plastic bag. Heat your oven to 220°C/420°F.

10. Brush with the glaze and bake for about half an hour. After the first 20 minutes, carefully open the oven door and glaze again. Without burning yourself: I couldn't live with that on my conscience…

recipes

The photographer

He always arrived a month before Christmas, and we knew exactly what to expect that afternoon: no running in the garden, no friends to play, a ban on toys, and a thorough grooming from Delfina: nails cut, hair done, smart clothes. We even had to do our homework in advance and miss out on children's TV, because at 4 o'clock on the dot – as if he'd eaten the alarm clock like the crocodile in Peter Pan – the doorbell rang and it would be him: the photographer.

He came with all his professional gear, a great heap of brown leather cases, that he placed on the dining room table with hieratic gestures. When someone came to work at our house their tools were usually hoes, trowels, drills, or at most paintbrushes, because our house was big and needed constant upkeep. It was impossible for us, three children all born within four years of each other, to maintain a respectful distance from our visitors, on such occasions. Gambucci the gardener let us use his garden tools, Venanzio the builder discovered that we had been using his plaster mix when our Das clay had run out, and even the painter – perhaps because he was Delfina's son – used to give us small tins of half dried wall paint, which we used to decorate big stones.

But with the photographer it was different. All those mysterious objects, that he dusted with a chamois leather and flicked with a small brush, were totally off-limits. All we could do was observe him, with our elbows on the table and our knees on the upholstered chair, while he adjusted his camera lenses as if he was Captain Hook busy with his pirate telescope. In absolute silence, or else - he said - we would distract him. Our house was big and cheerful, always full of noise and chatter: it had its own "melodies", which ranged from Delfina's shrilling when she discovered mud splatters on the floor, to Olaf's enthusiastic barking, and the ringing of our bicycle bells. But when the photographer came, even old Olaf was lost for words: he would wait in his basket, watching us and commiserating, wagging his tail impatiently.

I have no idea how it all began, or who had put the idea in our mother's head that we should be subjected to an afternoon of martyrdom in order to send Christmas wishes to our family and friends, but she wasn't the only one. In the run-up to Christmas, beautifully handwritten rectangular envelopes made with elegant paper arrived by post: inside were the faces of children we knew well - friends, cousins, the children of acquaintances - dressed for a party and smiling, printed in black and white on photographic paper. Typed copperplate writing would announce: "Luca, Giovanni and Marta wish you a very Merry Christmas and a Happy New Year!" Three wobbly signatures would follow, and it was easy to understand that their mother had written Marta's name, as she was only three, and that Luca, who was in Year 1, still couldn't write an "a" that didn't resemble a deflated balloon.

It was a small comfort knowing that we were not the only ones: we had fun comparing our photo cards

stories

14

with the others and suggesting hints of innovation to our mother, but she would never concede. Stylistic deviations such as shiny paper or a photomontage with Christmas baubles in the background would never have entered her head.

And so we were condemned, year after year, to sit in front of that fireplace. Mamma and the photographer had already decided it was the most festive spot in the house, and it didn't matter that we thought it was much more festive to be immortalised in an adventurous corner of the garden with our own toys instead. Well-worn and not altogether presentable, they would have been out of place. As a compromise, we brought with us three perfumed rubber Disney toys, which can now be seen in the window of the local antique shop because they've become collector's items: they came out well in black and white, discreet but cheerful without distracting too much from our smart outfits.

The Christmas look for children then consisted of a grey jumper (with the cuffs turned back, because good clothes had to last for more than a season), a skirt or short trousers made of Scottish wool (matching tartan for everyone, of course) to the knee, and long grey woollen socks inside little suede shoes (at the time children went around bare-legged and no-one ever got cold). There was no place for frivolities, the only exception being my sister's hair-do: she needed a little aesthetic assistance, due her lack of appetite and skinniness.

That particular year she had a small hairband of tiny velvet flowers in her hair. It had cost the earth and had come from the milliner's, which was a kind of boutique for ladies where you could find elegant gloves, ribbons and hats, too. Sitting on tweed cushions in front of the fireplace, we were getting even more bored than usual, or maybe we were just a little older than the previous year, and we had developed more of an enterprising spirit. A joke came into my brother's head, a harmless joke to scare my sister. She was the smallest of us, but she was already tough and quite fearless. Because she didn't eat, she was allowed to stay at home with Delfina, instead of going to the Montessori nursery school with us: she would happily go hunting in the garden (she had a passion for caterpillars) and play with the dog, and she obeyed only when she wanted to. Nothing scared her. Nothing, except the *Befana*…

In our house, Christmas always saw the arrival of the *Befana*, a good old witch, bent over from flying around the world on her broomstick through freezing winter skies, to deliver sweets and coal to good and bad children respectively. She would arrive at night, down the chimney stack. Not down any old fireplace (we had more than one in our house), but this particular one…

So, while the photographer set up his tripod and dusted and focused the lens once again, we thought we'd make her believe that we'd seen the *Befana* on the roof, and that we were sure she would come down the chimney any minute now: maybe she had more to do this Christmas, so she must have started her journey early.

It wasn't hard to make her believe it, making fun of her was easy, she was only three and a half and we were her two older mischievous siblings. Without the grown-ups hearing, we whispered "Befaaanaaa…" in her ear, menacingly, as if we were telling a spooky ghost story.

As a result of these terrifying whispers - in stereo, as she was sitting between us - she became breathless, her eyes and mouth wide open in terror as if pleading for help, but no words came out. Even the most expensive of velvet hairbands couldn't have tamed her black hair that stood on end in shock (and goodness knows how many different hairbands they had tried on in the shop, pretty much the whole drawer labelled "Velvet"): she was paralysed with fright. Shivers of fear went down her back (because the *Befana* would always grip you from behind, as soon as she came down the chimney) and she was frozen in the "shoulders straight!" position, that mothers like so much (they're always proud, and a little emotional, when their child sits up straight as a die, especially in public).

Well, no-one noticed a thing. While Cartier-Bresson was busy with his artistic shots, Mamma kept an eye from a distance so as not to distract him and warned us to stop sniggering, because the photos would come out all wobbly, and our grandparents would have to look at us being out of focus for a whole year. We had to sit up straight, like my sister: "She's the smallest of all of you, and look what a good girl she is today!"

The photographer left with his mountain of brown cases, and the certainty of having caught memorable images of his prey. Of course, there would have been the odd bad shot ("Madam, it's impossible to keep three children sitting still all at the same time!") and it was a shame, because one had to pay for and keep the bad shots, too. There would always be at least one worthy of printing, though: we just had to wait until they were developed, before heading to his shop to choose which image, font and wording were best. I ask you, how could that year's greeting have been any different from the previous years, seeing as the cards would be for grandparents, aunts, uncles and dear friends as usual? They knew us well, they saw us often, and so we didn't understand why they needed to see us arriving by post, too. Perhaps it made us more interesting being in black and white, and sitting still for a change.

That year, making the choice was a long and laborious task, even worse than choosing the velvet hairband at the milliner's. "I don't know how it could have happened..." the photographer said to our mother as he showed her the photos. There was not even one in which my sister didn't have her eyes crossed, her mouth wide open and her hair standing on end: she looked like a cat about to be run over by a lorry. The two children on either side of the fireplace wore similar features, but contrasting expressions: a look of mocking enjoyment, you could say...

The envelopes were ready, after all have you ever had Christmas without children's greetings cards? They were sent, full of signatures of trembling joined-up letters. But that was the last time Cartier-Bresson came to our house: no more afternoons spent in preparatory visits to the milliner's, or posing in front of the fireplace. What a relief!

My sister was always scared of the *Befana*, but she remained the most fearless of our trio: she carried on refusing to go to nursery school, hunting caterpillars and obeying only when she felt like it.
She became a beautiful young girl who was much romanced and very photogenic. And nowadays, in her house on the other side of the world, she doesn't have radiators: only a fireplace...

St Lucy's sweet buns

These have a wonderful aroma of orange and saffron. They are lovely plain, or with jam and a nice cup of tea. But do bear in mind the "mature cheese & cold cuts" option: most intriguing, as Principessa's friends claim…

TIME: 3½-4 HOURS

MAKES 20 ROLLS OR 2 WREATHS

300 g/10 oz bread flour
200 g/7 oz all-purpose flour
A pinch of salt
1 unwaxed orange
200 ml/6.5 fl oz fresh whipping
    cream
2 generous pinches saffron
80 g/just over 3 oz full fat yogurt
100 g/4 oz caster sugar
25 g/1 oz compressed fresh yeast
1 medium egg
20 g/just under 1 oz very soft butter
    (plus a knob to grease the bowl)
A handful of sultanas

FOR THE FINISHING
1 egg white, beaten with 2
    tablespoons water
2 tablespoons caster sugar

New to yeast cookery?
Instructions on p.186!

1. In a large bowl, whisk together the flours and salt and make a well in the centre. Rinse and dry the orange, then grate the zest directly into the bowl (do not mix: risk of lumps!).

2. Warm the cream, just below boiling, add the saffron and allow to cool. Then add 1 tablespoon yogurt, 1 tablespoon sugar and 2 heaped tablespoons flour taken from the respective totals, as well as the crumbled yeast. Mix to break up any lumps and leave to rise in a warm place for about 15 minutes until doubled in volume. In the meantime, break the egg and beat gently. Add the rest of the sugar to the flour.

3. Pour the yeast into the bowl with the flour, add the egg and the remaining 2 tablespoons of yogurt. Mix with a spoon until it becomes hard to stir, then use your hands: pinch a part of the dough from the edge, stretch it outwards, then fold it back into the center. Turn the bowl a few degrees, pinch another part of the dough and repeat the movement. Continue with these stretches and folds for a few minutes, until the ingredients are evenly mixed.

4. Transfer your dough onto the worktop , and knead with the "snakes & snails" technique (see p. 186), stretching and rolling the dough for 12 times (no more than 10 minutes). It shouldn't be too sticky, but don't add any more flour: grease your hands and worktop generously with butter and keep doing this between one twist and another (you need to incorporate all the butter).

5. Place the dough back into the clean and freshly buttered bowl, seal with cling film and leave to rise until doubled in volume (it will take about an hour and a half). In the meantime, soak the sultanas in a bowl of warm water.

6. Line a baking tray with parchment paper. Turn your dough out onto the worktop, divide it in half and place one half under the upturned bowl. Cut the other half into 10 pieces, roll into small snakelike shapes about 25 cm/9.5" long, then curl the ends in opposite directions to form a "S". Place them on the tray separately if you wish them to lead an autonomous life, or side by side if you wish to make a wreath. Place sultanas into the centre of each coil of dough (tuck them in well or they'll escape!).

7. Put the tray into a large, inflated, well secured plastic bag and allow to rise for 15-20 minutes. Preheat your oven to 220°C/420°F. Beat the egg white gently with 2 tablespoons of water.

8. Brush with the glaze, sprinkle over some sugar and bake for 15-20 minutes. Transfer to a cooling rack by lifting it on its parchment paper, and allow to cool before adding a bow. And don't forget that you have another 10 buns still under the bowl, waiting to go in the oven…

Kugelhupf

Kugelhupf is the best companion for a cup of hot chocolate. All you need to decide is if you'll have those crunchy almonds to start, or save them until the end…

TIME: 3½ HOURS

FOR A BUNDT TIN 22 CM/ 8.5" IN DIAMETER

250 g/10 oz bread flour
100 g/4 oz all-purpose flour
A pinch of salt
100 ml/3 fl oz milk
60 g/just over 2 oz caster sugar
2 medium eggs
80 g/just over 3 oz soft butter (plus a knob to grease the tin)
12 g/½ oz compressed fresh yeast
120 g/just under 5 oz sultanas
Peeled almonds

FOR THE FINISHING
1 tablespoon melted butter

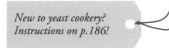

New to yeast cookery? Instructions on p.186!

1. Take the butter and the eggs out of the fridge first (the butter needs to be soft). Rinse the sultanas and soak them in warm water.
Generously butter the tin and place an almond in each groove.

2. In a large bowl, whisk together the flours and salt and make a well in the centre.

3. Gently warm the milk. Add 1 tablespoon sugar and 2 heaped tablespoons flour taken from the respective totals, and the crumbled yeast. Mix until you get a smooth, dense consistency then leave to rise in a warm place for about 15 minutes: it should double in volume.

4. While the yeast is resting (or rather, working) separate the eggs. Whip the whites until stiff with the sugar (as stiff as if you are making meringues).

5. Pour the yeast mixture into the bowl with the flour, without mixing (be delicate, treat the yeast it as if it's a sleeping new born baby), cover with the whipped egg whites and then a layer of flour taken from the edges, without breaking the central well. Leave to rest for another 15 minutes.

6. In the meantime beat the egg yolks lightly. Then add to the other ingredients, and mix with a spoon until the dough just holds together. Now take a ⅓ of the butter, spread it all over the dough and begin to knead inside the bowl: pinch a part of the dough from the edge, stretch it outwards, then fold it back into the center. Turn the bowl a few degrees, pinch another part of the dough and repeat the movement. Continue with these stretches and folds for a few minutes, until the ingredients are evenly mixed.

7. Transfer the dough onto the worktop, and continue adding butter as you use the "grab-beat-fold" technique for 200 folds. Butter the worktop and your hands generously, while you're working: when you have finished, there should be no butter left.

8. Squeeze out of the sultanas and spread them out around the dough (dry your hands, as even the smallest amount of dampness is enough to make the dough unmanageable). Roll the dough over the sultanas, making sure you catch them all; then stretch and fold it gently, so that the sultanas are evenly distributed. Now shape a ball, create a hole with your finger in the middle and enlarge it until you form a ring (it won't be smooth and perfect, the dough is quite sticky but that's fine). Place the ring on the bottom of the tin without moving it too much, so that the almonds which you positioned so lovingly and precisely will remain in place. Allow to rise in a large, inflated, well secured plastic bag, until the dough reaches the top of the tin (about an hour and a half or two hours).

9. When it is almost ready, preheat your oven to 200°C/400°F. Brush the kugelhupf with the melted butter just before it goes in the oven, and bake for 30-40 minutes. Leave to cool for 5 minutes in the tin, then remove and place on a cooling rack.

Sapa bread with sultanas, spices and orange

Sapa is wine must cooked until it has the consistency of syrup. It has an aroma all of its own, stronger than bitter honey, sweeter than balsamic vinegar: the very scent of winter. It goes well with cheeses and dried fruit, as well as in this lovely bread, that smells of orange, sultanas, cloves and cinnamon, too. Don't be fooled, it's not a sweet brioche but a black bread with a Nordic influence. It's the perfect travelling companion to cheese and chutney, but also to smoked herrings and cucumber. It lasts for days, if you leave it cut side down on a wooden chopping board. And when it hardens, it works well as a lightly toasted base for various toppings.

TIME: 3½ HOURS + OVERNIGHT
RESTING IN THE FRIDGE

300 g/10 oz bread flour
150 g/6 oz wholemeal rye flour
1 heaped teaspoon powdered
   cinnamon
1 heaped teaspoon powdered cloves
A pinch of salt
1 unwaxed orange
100 g/4 oz sultanas
50 ml/1.7 fl oz sapa
150 ml/5 fl oz water
50 g/2 oz muscovado sugar
40 g/just under 2 oz butter
   (plus a knob to grease the bowl)
80 g/just over 3 oz full fat yogurt
25 g/1 oz compressed fresh yeast

*New to yeast cookery?
Instructions on p.186!*

1. In a large bowl, whisk together the flours, cinnamon, cloves and salt and make a well in the centre. Rinse and dry the orange, grate the zest directly into the bowl (do not mix: we want no lumps, here...).

2. Soak the sultanas in a bowl of warm water.

3. In a small pan warm the sapa, water and sugar without boiling. Switch off the hob, add the butter and, when it has melted, add the yogurt and the crumbled yeast (check that the liquid is just warm); mix well to dissolve the yeast, and pour straight into the bowl with the flour.

4. Mix with a spoon until it becomes hard to stir, then get your hands in and knead until the ingredients are evenly mixed.

5. Transfer your dough onto the worktop, and knead with the "snakes & snails" technique (see p. 186), stretching and rolling the dough for about 10 times (or about 10 minutes). If it's very sticky and unmanageable, leave it for 10 minutes under the upturned bowl before starting. Squeeze out the sultanas and spread them out around the dough. Roll the dough over them, making sure you catch them all. Then stretch and fold it gently to ensure the sultanas reach right inside the dough.

6. Place the dough back in a clean bowl greased with butter, seal with cling film and leave in the fridge overnight: it will have all the necessary time to rise slowly. It won't rise a lot, but don't let this worry you.

7. The next morning, remove it from the fridge and leave it for an hour at room temperature before shaping it. Flatten it delicately, take the outer edges and close them into the middle to make a sort of bundle; turn it (seam side down) and shape into a round loaf, by caressing it with your hands. Place it on a baking tray lined with parchment paper, and allow to rise until doubled in volume, inside a large, inflated, well-secured plastic bag (it will take about an hour).

8. Bake at 220°C/420°F (preheat your oven) for 25-30 minutes. It will stay fresh for several days.

❄ *If you have a cast iron pot, use it as an "oven within an oven" to bake this bread. Put it, lid on, in the preheated oven for 15 minutes, then wear your oven mitts and remove it (be careful not to burn yourself!). Pop the bread inside with its parchment paper, close it straightaway and bake for 25-30 minutes. Then take the bread out of the pot, lifting it on its parchment paper and continue baking for another 5 minutes on the oven grill shelf.*

recipes

Panettone with walnuts and gorgonzola

Have fun dressing up this savoury brioche dough as a panettone, and serve it with cheese and cold cuts, or on its own, as an appetizer: in both cases, it will benefit from a glass of wine... and you, too. If you can't find a panettone case (the traditional, unmistakeable paper one), use a round brioche tin or a rectangular loaf tin.

Time: 4 hours

Makes a panettone of 15 cm/6"
in diameter + a small loaf

100 g/4 oz sultanas
100 g/4 oz walnuts
300 g/12 oz bread flour
150 g/6 oz all-purpose flour
1 tablespoon salt
120 ml/4 fl oz milk
1 tablespoon honey
80 g/just over 3 oz full fat yogurt
25 g/1 oz compressed fresh yeast
50 g/2 oz butter (plus a knob to work
    the dough and grease the bowl)
150 g/5 oz gorgonzola cheese
2 medium eggs

For the finishing
1 tablespoon melted butter

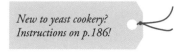

New to yeast cookery?
Instructions on p.186!

❄ *With these quantities*
   you'll produce a dough that
is too big for the indicated mould.
Use the remaining portion (a
third of the total) to make a
small loaf. Given the reduced
dimensions, it will rise more
quickly than the panettone, so the
little loaf has the right of way on
the road to the oven.

1. Soak the sultanas in a bowl of warm water. Toast the walnuts in a non-stick pan. Once cool, break them up with your hands, then put a few at a time into a sieve and shake to remove the skins (they can burn easily).

2. In a large bowl, whisk together the flours and salt and make a well in the centre. Warm the milk gently, then add the honey, yogurt, 1 heaped tablespoon of flour taken from the total, and the crumbled yeast. Mix to break up any lumps and leave to rise in a warm place for about 15 minutes: it should double in volume.

3. In the meantime, melt the butter over a low heat; add the gorgonzola in chunks and stir to allow the cheese to melt a little: it shouldn't be completely melted down, but just soft. If a few pieces remain, that's fine.
Break the eggs and gently beat them.

4. Pour the yeast mixture into the bowl with the flours, add the butter and gorgonzola mixture, and the eggs; mix until the dough holds together. It's a very sticky dough at this stage, so work with a spoon until it becomes hard to stir. Then grease one hand with butter and begin to knead inside the bowl: pinch a part of the dough from the edge, stretch it outwards, then fold it back into the center. Turn the bowl a few degrees, pinch another part of the dough and repeat the movement. Continue with these stretches and folds for 5 minutes.

5. Transfer the dough onto the buttered worktop, and leave under the upturned bowl for 10 minutes. Then butter your hands and worktop (yes, again...) and use the "grab-beat-fold" technique for 200 folds. Don't add more flour: use butter when the dough becomes unmanageable. But know that it's one of those "sticky to the bitter end" doughs, so resign yourself to the idea and... go forth! Once kneaded, roll it over the walnuts and squeezed-out sultanas, stretching and folding it gently over and over until all the ingredients are incorporated.

6. Place the dough back into the clean and freshly buttered bowl, cover with cling film, and leave to rise until doubled in volume (about an hour and a half).

7. Gentlly deflate the dough. It will still be sticky, so handle it as little as possible using buttered hands: take two-thirds, shape into a ball and put it into your panettone case. Then put the whole thing into a large, inflated, well-secured plastic bag and leave it to rise until doubled in volume (about 45 minutes). When it is almost ready, preheat the oven to 220°C/420°F, and lower the grill shelf so that the panettone fits inside.

8. Delicately brush with butter, and score a cross in the top (a razor blade is the right utensil: use gently!). Bake for 30-40 minutes. If you see that it is browning too much, cover it with a sheet of aluminium foil. Once out of the oven, push a knitting needle through your panettone, and keep it top-down until it has completely cooled (in this way it will maintain its voluptuous silhouette!). Keep it in a plastic bag or wrapped in foil: it will stay fresh for a few days.

Pain d'épices

A true pain d'épices doesn't have yeast, or butter or eggs, not even obscure, mysterious ingredients: only rye flour, honey and scent of spices. If you respect its nature, it acquires its creamy consistency, keeps well and can be transformed – depending on the occasion – into a slice of cake to accompany tea or into the perfect companion to a piece of cheese (ever tried crostini with gorgonzola and plum compôte?). If you keep it wrapped in parchment paper and cling film, it will last for several days: you'll have ample time to experiment, and decide which option ranks no. 1 on your personal rating list. If, like me, you have a friend who would do pretty much anything for a slice of pain d'épices, wrap it (the bread, not your friend) in some beautiful paper and create a gift. Finally, for accuracy's sake: the two spoonfuls of black treacle that give it an unmistakeable flavour are the idea of Cedric's mother, who ended up in France for love, all the way from Connecticut. Perhaps it is not so French but if you can manage to add it you'll realise that a wise cultural contamination is greatly enriching...

TIME: 1 HOUR

FOR A 10 X 20 CM/3" X 8" TIN

100 g/4 oz all-purpose flour
150 g/6 oz wholemeal rye flour
3-4 teaspoons four spices mix
200 ml/7 fl oz water
250 g/8 oz honey
2 tablespoons black treacle
1 level teaspoon bicarbonate of soda
A pinch of salt

1. Preheat the oven to 180°C/350°F. Line a pullman tin with parchment paper, so that 2-3cm/0.8-1" paper hangs over the edge (you'll need this to lift the pain d'épices from the tin once it is cooked).

2. Mix the flours together in a bowl with the four spices mixture.

3. In a small pan heat the water with honey and black treacle; it mustn't get too hot, just over body temperature (you should dip a finger in and hardly notice the difference).

4. Off the hob, add the bicarbonate of soda with the salt to the liquids, mix straightaway and... be prepared to a little effervescence! Salt and bicarbonate of soda produce an explosion of foam in no time at all.
Pour this immediately into the bowl with the flours and mix rapidly with a spoon until the dough is homogenous. Be quick, as quick as you can.

5. Scrape the dough into the tin, level with the back of the spoon and bake immediately. The pain d'èpices should be baked for 35-40 minutes, without becoming too dry. Touch it: it should be a little rubbery but without traces of raw dough on the top.

6. Lift the bread out of the tin, holding the sides of the parchment paper firmly, and place it on a plate; fold over the edges of the paper to wrap it up, and cover it with a clean tea towel as if sheltering it from a snowstorm. Truthfully, you only need to protect it from drying out: any dampness is precious, as it keeps the bread soft, so you mustn't allow it to escape. Now that you know this little secret, try to keep it safe: pain d'épices doesn't like open air. Once completely cool, replace the cloth with a few layers of cling film, without removing the parchment paper. If you can guarantee it this comfy clothing, it'll last for days. Just be careful to ensure it is totally cool before the outfit change: if you see steam forming under its waterproof cling film new coat, go back to the breathable cloth one, and postpone the seasonal wardrobe changeover!

❄ *A pullman loaf tin (lid off) will guarantee you a perfectly shaped pain d'épices. If you don't have one, you can just as easily use a plumcake tin: you'll have slightly more trapezoidal slices, but the flavour will be just as good. After all, "beauty is imperfection"...*

Paulina's sapa and walnut cake

Yet another page out of Paulina's notebook… She generously lends me her family recipes: when I taste them I'm always spellbound, and I have to ask her for a piece of paper and a pencil. This cake of hers is similar to the rye and dates one which Gudrun – half-German, half-Danish – gave to me when she came for Italian lessons. They are similar in winter aroma, flavour and atmosphere, and even though they come from places several hundred kilometres apart, they contend for first prize in "The-perfect-spiced-cake-to-go-with-a-nice-hot-cup-of-tea" competition. Truthfully, Paulina sometimes prepares this cake for the beach, too, and no-one has ever complained. These are only trivialities, or rather "fripperies!", as her gourmet consort would say. How can he be wrong? There's absolutely no reason why you shouldn't eat a cake that smells of sapa after a good swim. By the way, where we go swimming the water's freezing…

TIME: 1½ HOURS + 15 MINUTES
FOR GLAZING

MAKES A 22 CM/9" DIAMETER CAKE

150-200 g/6-8 oz crushed walnuts
80 g/just over 3 oz butter (plus a
   knob to grease the tin)
200 ml/7 fl oz sapa
150 g/6 oz unrefined cane sugar
2 large eggs
300 g/12 oz all-purpose flour (plus
   1 tablespoon for the tin)
1 unwaxed orange
1 unwaxed lemon
150-200 g/5-7 oz sultanas
1 sachet baking powder
100 ml/3 fl oz milk

FOR THE FINISHING
200 g/7 oz icing sugar
1 egg white
The juice of ½ a lemon

1. Preheat your oven to 180°C/350°F. Grease the tin with butter, then dust with flour and tap out the excess.

2. Rinse the sultanas and put them in a bowl of warm water. Melt the butter on a low heat.

3. Toast the walnuts in a non-stick pan. Once cool, break them up with your hands, then put a few at a time into a sieve and shake to remove the skins (they can burn easily).

4. Break the eggs into a large bowl, add the sugar and whisk with an electric hand mixer for a few minutes: stop when the mixture is almost tripled in volume, pale and thick enough to leave a ribbon trail on the surface when the whisk is lifted.

5. Pour the melted butter and sapa into the bowl and mix well. Add the grated citrus zest and the flour, a third at a time, continuing to whisk until you get a homogenous mixture. Then add the milk, in which you have dissolved the yeast (do this just before you need it).

6. Finally, add the walnuts and the squeezed-out sultanas, mix with a spoon (no whisking here, so as not to ruin them) and tip into the tin. Level out and bake for 40-45 minutes. Leave the cake in the tin for 5 minutes, before placing it on a cooling rack.

7. When it is cool, prepare the glaze. Gently beat the egg white with a fork (you don't need to whip it, only break it). In a medium bowl, combine the sugar and egg white and work with a rubber spatula, adding the lemon juice a little at a time (you probably won't need all of it): the glaze will become perfectly smooth in about a minute. Let it fall over the cake (it's amazing!) and if by chance it hadn't the courage to dive into the grooves, help it with the back of a spoon. Leave it to solidify (it will take about an hour) and then decorate it as you please: candied fruit, walnut kernels, silver balls, or an improvised wreath of whatever you have available. You'll only need to put some berries and a few little fir branches (or rosemary ones…) in the egg white, then some caster sugar and… it would look like a snowfall had made your cake all the more beautiful!

The
biscuit tin

The flying capon

It usually arrived at our house with Delfina, in a wooden box tied with string to the luggage rack of her scooter. The upgrade to a Lambretta was all her doing, studied right down to the tiniest detail so that it could hold bigger animals: she could have stuck chickens and rabbits on the handlebars, but a capon… well, that would have made her swerve at the first corner! The rough road leading from her farmyard to the town was full of holes, stones and ditches, and with the arrival of winter and snow she had already ended up with her legs in the air, on more than one occasion.

So we went to pick it up from her house. Every time we went to that small farm in the countryside it was like a trip to the fair: cows, rabbits to stroke, the sty with the sow and her piglets, which made our mother take leave of her senses, but we adored them…We were as high as kites on the journey home, so we would sing our little hearts out.

Mamma found ingenious ways to make us behave in the car. Three children in the back of a tiny Fiat 500 – in the days before seat belts or child car seats – would have driven even Manuel Fangio round the bend. She had various tricks up her sleeve, including reading registration numbers (all three of us learned to read doing this), pretending to drive along with her ("Come on children! Sharp bend to the riiiiiight!" and all of us would turn our imaginary steering wheel…vrooom!), or thinking of as many words as possible beginning with a particular letter ("Now think of words beginning with p!", and we began with pig and petunia, and ended with poop: at that point a stern glance shot back in our direction from the driver's mirror, and we would carry on with the next letter).

However, that particular day we quickly got tired of singing. None of us felt like driving or making a string of words, so we were allowed to do what we usually couldn't: kneel on the back seat and look out of the rear window, to wave to the drivers behind us. You should know that in those days, now and again you would see cars decorated as if they were living rooms. Some had a crocheted rug carefully placed over the back seat, others had patterned cushions, or even an array of plastic dogs curled up on the back shelf: because they were examples of the species "Bobble-head plastic dog" ("Canis plasticus automatopoetus"), their heads nodded every time the car went over a bump, and it seemed that they were really barking. Well, that afternoon we seemed to be just like those springy dogs, that we would have loved to have in our car but our mother wouldn't even consider buying them, independent of the fact that we already had our very real – and very big – dog in the garden at home.
"Children, don't distract the driver…"
"OK, Mamma" (multiplied by three), even though the driver must have already been distracted enough: it would be distracting for anyone if three little gnomes appeared at the back of the car in front, all wearing the same blue duffle coats buttoned up to the neck, woollen mittens and red bobble hats…

Anyway, we managed to behave and refrain from making funny faces, but suddenly people in the cars behind us started making signs.

"Mamma, why is everyone waving at us today?"
"Because they're being polite, you should always wave…"
A bend to the right, and the bobble hat trio sways together in the opposite direction. The car straightens up again and so do they. The journey continues smoothly.
"Mamma, there's a man who's waving at us a lot…"
"Well, he can see how nice you all are! Why don't you smile and wave back?"
A double bend, and the little car careers left then right, with the trio in the back following suit. Everybody straightens up once more, one puts his bobble hat back in position as it has slipped over his eyes.
A steep hill, crossroads, a sharp brake and… stop! A red light that seems to last forever, because Christmas is just round the corner and there's a lot of traffic.

It was a gorgeous winter afternoon, the sky a silvery grey full of light from the falling snow. Great big snowflakes landed on the windscreen, only to be scraped aside in an instant by the wipers: swish! swash! then others took their place. At last we were in the city. The lights came on one by one, the grey faded into purple, and the snowflakes formed a soft layer on the tarmac.

"Mamma, it's great today: everyone is waving at us, even people who are walking!"
"That's the magic of Christmas, my love…"
"Wow! It's fantastic…"

We made our way home through crowds of cheering people, everyone waved their hands along our route. It was like the Queen's carriage on parade: they waved and we waved back. Smiling politely, and wearing woolly mittens. It's incredible how things can be so different with the magic of Christmas… it was a march of triumph!

It was when the lights turned green that everything – despite the purple sky and all that snow – became clear. The road was steep, we didn't have snow chains on our tyres, well… let's say that the clutch and gears were having a merry dance. The little Fiat 500 was off with a roar of its engine, it lurched forward and…
"Beep! Beep!" "Beebeep!" "Beeeeep!"
From all four corners of the crossroads, horns sounded in unison. All the cars stayed where they were, except ours. My mother was in shock, she looked in the mirror and then… she saw it.

In the middle of the crossroads, a newly-plucked capon lay in the snow. Having journeyed for a while on the roof of the car in falling snow, without even wearing hat and mittens, it was visibly freezing to the bone. Well, let's say half-frozen.

It was gathered up by a certain elegant lady, who, having a good sense of humour, retained her composure. She got nonchalantly out of her car, confidently grabbed it by its legs, and stuck it in the boot.
From the rear window, three little gnomes were watching her and sniggering: they were wearing blue coats buttoned up to the neck, woollen mittens and red bobble hats. They never stopped waving at people who were observing the scene: because you always have to be polite. And because this, too, is the magic of Christmas…

stories

33

Tree biscuits with spices and cocoa

Christmas wouldn't be Christmas without a fresh batch of biscuits to hang on the tree! It's such fun preparing them and it really doesn't matter if the quality controllers decide to nibble a few straightaway with the excuse that they're a bit dribbly or have wonky holes: Advent Sundays were made for baking cookies.
Get the children to join in. Or rather, let your own inner child run free…

Time: 2 hours (for 2 batches, excluding decoration time)

Makes about 60 biscuits

For the dough
150 g/6 oz cold butter in cubes
1 large egg
2 tablespoons black treacle
300 g/12 oz all-purpose flour
120 g/5 oz muscovado sugar
10 g/½ oz sifted dark cocoa powder
2 teaspoons four spice mix
A large pinch of salt

For the finishing
1 tablet white chocolate

1. Cut the butter into cubes and put it back in the fridge until you need to use it. In a small bowl, beat the egg a little with the black treacle.

2. Put the flour, sugar, sifted cocoa, four spice mix and salt in a mixer. Blend for a moment, just to mix them a bit. Add the butter and blend again intermittently until you get a sandy consistency.

3. Add the egg and black treacle mixture and continue to blend at 10 second intervals to avoid warming the ingredients: stop as soon as it all comes together. If it seems too dry, add 1 or 2 spoonfuls of cold water (but try not to go overboard, you need to be able to roll it out easily).

4. Place the dough onto a sheet of parchment paper, flatten it out with your hands making it into a large omelette (don't squash it too much), then cover with another sheet and widen it a little with a rolling pin (you don't need to reach the final thickness now, but you can work in advance to make further flattening later on easier). Transfer it to the fridge for a quarter of an hour.

5. Heat the oven to 180°C/350°F and line a baking tray with parchment paper.

6. Roll the dough out to 4mm/almost ½", keeping it between the 2 sheets of parchment paper. This is to avoid adding flour: that would leave snowy traces all over the biscuit surface. The only snow forecast, at this stage, is reserved for the edging of the biscuits: dip the biscuit cutter in flour between one cut and another, if you're aiming for a perfect shape. Later the white chocolate will remove any further trace of flour…
Transfer the biscuits to the baking tray without worrying to distance them too much (there's no baking powder so they won't expand on cooking). When the tray is full, pop it back in the fridge for a quarter of an hour.

7. Make a hole in each biscuit, bake for ten minutes then remove them from the oven, turn them and put them back for another five minutes. Allow to cool on a cooling rack.

8. Melt the chocolate over a bain-marie, wait for it to cool down a bit (otherwise it would run too much), then put it into a piping bag and decorate the biscuits. You'll have to wait a few hours before you can hang them on the tree dribble-free…

❄ *Making holes in the biscuits is a seriously zen activity: it requires calm, patience, precision and perfect self-control.*
It also calls for the right utensil, if available. If you have a very small diameter nozzle for a piping bag, use that: it's the right utensil. It produces regular holes and the piece of dough that comes away ends up in its cone, you only have to shake it off. If you don't have a piping nozzle, you don't need to give up your project. There's another more simple hole-making utensil that always works: see if you have a piece of vermicelli pasta (12 minutes cooking time!) and proceed. If the dough is cool enough it'll work like a dream!

recipes

Peppar-brun-biscotti

I adore biscuit tins, in fact I have quite a collection. I keep labels, ribbons and small candles inside them, as well as a store of incandescent light bulbs (I know, they're not exactly energy saving, but they have a soft light like no other, so I bought up shop-loads when they went out of production). Round biscuit tins have a unique characteristic, they're nearly all the same diameter so they can be stacked easily: this is especially useful if you decide to fill your cupboards with them! For years I bought Ikea spiced biscuits because I wanted the tins. No-one really liked the biscuits themselves, but the tins with little gnomes on the top have become part of our Christmas tradition. It's lovely coming face-to-face with an authentic Scandinavian gnome, whenever you change a light bulb throughout the year!
I finally came up with my own spiced biscuit recipe, so that I could manage to fill the tins with food, especially for celebration days. It's a combination of Swedish papparkakor, Danish brunkager, Belgian speculaas, and Brigitta's biscuits I used to make as a child by following Grandma Duck's Handbook.
Even if it's been hard to find a name that would be pronounceable in Italian, at last I created biscuits that everyone loves! They're wholewheat enough and deliciously crunchy. They have the aroma of toasted almonds, a little touch of spice (perfect, even if you don't usually "walk on the spice side"), and lots of cane sugar: the really dark, aromatic type. So, throw yourself into biscuit production, with the excuse of filling every tin you possess! As to the name, you decide. It depends on the variations that you make to the recipe. We call them peppar-brun-biscotti: I'd love to know what you decide to call yours...

TIME: 1 HOUR 45 MINUTES
(FOR 2 BATCHES) + RESTING IN
THE FRIDGE

MAKES 30-35 BISCUITS

70 g/just under 3 oz peeled almonds
100 g/4 oz all-purpose flour
70 g/just under 3 oz whole-weat
    wheat flour
50 g/2 oz unrefined cane sugar
½ coffeespoon bicarbonate of soda
A large pinch of salt
1 level tablespoon four spice mix
A small piece of fresh ginger
60 g/just over 2 oz butter
1 medium egg
2 tablespoons golden syrup

1. Toast the almonds, allow to cool and cut each one into 2-3 pieces. Put them in a bowl with the flours, sugar, sifted bicarbonate of soda, salt and the four spice mix; combine well.
Peel, rinse and dry the ginger, then grate it directly in the bowl without mixing (otherwise it will cling to the flour and form lumps).

2. Melt the butter and leave to cool; add the golden syrup and the egg, beat with a fork and pour it into the bowl with the dry ingredients.

3. Mix with a spoon until the dough comes together, then work it with your hands in the bowl for no more than a minute: stop as soon as it becomes homogenous (you need to avoid warming it if you want your biscuits to be crumbly and fragrant).

4. Put it on the worktop and make a 20 cm/8" long roll. Wrap it in cling film and try to keep it compact so that no holes remain inside and the outside is as smooth as possible. Put it in the fridge for a few hours or, even better, a night (the colder it is, the easier it will be to cut).

5. When you decide to cook the biscuits, preheat the oven to 180°C/350°F and line a baking tray with parchment paper. Cut the roll into 3-4mm/½" slices with a sharp knife; place them on the tray with a little distance between each one (they'll expand on cooking), and put them back in the fridge for 15 minutes. Remove and bake for 7-8 minutes, then turn the biscuits over and continue baking for another 5 minutes (you will have 2 batches).

6. They'll be soft when you take them out of the oven, so let them cool before you try them. If you wish them to be deliciously fragrant, keep them in a tin: with a gnome on the top if possible...

Butter, sugar and almond stars

"Mala tempora currunt" (bad times are upon us) the butter would say if it could talk. It's always number one in the list of banned ingredients by the Gastro-Penitents World League. Now, if it's true that transgression is a corollary of pleasure (a philosophy that can extend to other fields of human existence we won't talk about here…), it's easy to understand why the poor butter is permanently at the top of the sinful food hit parade. Let's say it: butter is delicious, "ontologically delicious" as a philosopher would say. That is a source of absolute pleasure for our taste buds. So, under this premise, don't you think it would be right to make the most of Christmas by using it a little more often? Butter won't be offended if it doesn't hear from you much in the following months: real friendship can withstand the test of time. The recipe is a cross between Danish finskbrod (who knows why they're known as "Finnish" biscuits in Denmark), Scottish shortbread, and the fruit pie pastry which is all the rage in our house. All three have an unmistakable aroma. Of butter, of course…

TIME: 2 HOURS (FOR 2 BATCHES)

MAKES ABOUT 50 BISCUITS

FOR THE DOUGH
250 g/8 oz soft butter
100 g/4 oz caster sugar
1 level teaspoon salt
350 g/14 oz all-purpose flour

FOR THE FINISHING
50 g/2 oz finely chopped toasted
   almonds
1 egg white
2 tablespoons caster sugar
½ teaspoon salt

❄ *Hazelnuts and almonds that have been toasted at home have a much better flavour than store-bought ones. This is also true for chopped nuts: if they haven't been stored well – it happens, sometimes – they completely lose their fragrance. So I strongly recommend that you toast your nuts and break them up with a meat pounder (an electric mixer would turn them into powder). As soon as you have the time, prepare small batches of good almonds and hazelnuts when available. Keep the chopped nuts in a glass jar.*

1. Cut the butter into cubes and keep it at room temperature until it becomes soft (not completely melted, just soft to the touch).
Preheat the oven to 180°C/350°F and line a baking tray with parchment paper.

2. Put the butter, sugar and salt into a mixer and blend at medium speed, scraping the sides often with a rubber spatula so that the mixture stays within the blades. Continue for a few minutes: the butter should become fluffy and soft with the sugar well combined (without dissolving).

3. Add the flour, 3-4 spoonfuls at a time, using the rubber spatula when necessary. When you have finished, place the dough on the worktop, gently press it down with your hands, make a ball and then let it have a refreshing break in the fridge for 15 minutes in a bowl sealed with cling film.

4. Once out of the fridge, roll out the dough with a rolling pin on a worktop that has been lightly dusted with flour, to 5-6mm/0.2" in height (so just a little higher than a baking powder dough). Cut the biscuits into the shapes you prefer. Beware of choosing strange shapes though, it's not such a great idea to bring out your most adventurous cutters as you're using an extremely soft rich buttery dough…
If you like a challenge, though, then use the magic of Christmas to help you, but remember to work quickly and handle the dough as little as possible (it will remain weak, even after a little time out in fresh air…), and dip your cutter in flour before each cut.

5. Put the biscuits back in the fridge for 15 minutes, then brush them with the egg white that you have beaten with 2 spoonfuls of water just before. Sprinkle with toasted almonds followed by the sugar and salt (previously mixed). Bake for 15-20 minutes. When you bring them out of the oven they'll still be soft, so don't touch them if you want them to keep their shape. Wait about 10 minutes before lifting them delicately and putting them to dry on a cooling rack.

Walnut amaretti

The technique is the same as for traditional amaretti – balls of sugar, egg white and nuts left to dry the night before baking – but the almonds have been replaced with walnuts. The result, using cane sugar, is quite different to the original: not as sweet, crunchy and very aromatic. This is for absolute beginners, so you'll manage to make them perfectly the first time, but if you decide to practise with the technique, Christmas is the ideal time to do it with the excuse of making the biscuits for friends!

Time: 1 hour 15 minutes + a
night for drying (excluding
decoration time)

Makes 20 biscuits

For the dough
150 g/ 6 oz walnut pieces
150 g/ 6 oz dark cane sugar (plus
about 80g/just over 3 oz
for dusting)
1 medium egg white

For the finishing
1 tablet white chocolate

1. Line a baking tray with parchment paper.

2. Toast the walnuts, leave them to cool then break them up with your hands. Put them in the mixer with the sugar and blitz at intervals of a few seconds (they mustn't get hot otherwise they'll become oily). Stop when you have obtained a rough "flour".

3. Whip the egg white until stiff (as we all know, it won't do as it's told unless it is completely free of yolk). Don't even think of using an electric whisk with such a small quantity: it'll only take you a few minutes by hand.

4. Gradually add the walnut and sugar "flour". Let it fall slowly, a couple of spoonfuls at a time and mix it with the egg white, using big movements so as not to break down the egg white. A rubber spatula is best for this, but if you don't have one, a spoon is just as good (but please buy the first rubber spatula you can find, it's a great investment).

5. Now lay down the spatula and arm yourself with a teaspoon. Use it to take small pieces of the dough and transform them into little balls with a diameter of 3cm/just over 1". As they are ready, pop them in a small bowl with the sugar, roll them around a little then place them on the baking tray, with some space between them as they expand on cooking. Leave to rest overnight without covering: they just need to dry.

6. Bake the biscuits in a preheated oven at 180°C/350°F for about 20 minutes: don't bake them for any longer than necessary or they'll become hard. They will still be very soft when you bring them out of the oven (your finger will sink if you touch them) so let them cool completely before decorating with the chocolate which you have melted in a bain-marie.

❄ *It is important that the walnuts are cold before you chop them with the sugar, otherwise the mixture will be damp and lumpy. If you are in a hurry, toast them in advance: you'll avoid lump risk and also save about half an hour of the time indicated! Breaking up the walnuts before putting them in the mixer also saves time and lumps caused by overheating: don't miss out this vital stage.*
As far as types of cane sugar are concerned, they are not all the same (and in fact, why should they be, given that "variety is the spice of life"). Some – such as muscovado, dark brown sugar and certain unrefined sugars – are quite damp: if you observe them closely it looks as if the grains are moving! They seem to stick together and drag each other in perpetual motion. These sugars are delicious, but not good for this recipe: if you add them to the mixer with the walnuts, they won't produce a really dry "flour" and you'll find yourself in the aforementioned situation. So choose a cane sugar that moves like caster sugar: that is just when you touch it (or stir it, or shake it, or...). If the grains are very large, put them in the mixer before adding the walnuts.

recipes

The bingo table
Crunchy stuff
and delicious nibbles

CROCCANTE
di
SESAMO

Almond brittle...

In brittle, shape and substance move along parallel lines: independent of the appearance you decide to give it, the taste will remain the same. This will depend on the quality of the almonds you've chosen, the amount of toasting they have had (burning them doesn't help) and your ability to judge the subtle difference between caramelised sugar and a caramel that is about to burn (a question of seconds: keep your eyes, nose and ears on red alert). A party outfit makes everyone look great, brittles included: it is Christmas after all! So if you have some extra time to try this out, please do, if only to extract an "oooh!" of wonder from your friends... Get yourself one or two sizeable metal biscuit cutters (it would be impossible to work with more, as the mixture starts to harden straightaway). Choose simple shapes. Grease the inside of the biscuit cutter with a layer of odourless oil (such as sunflower oil), and eliminate any excess with kitchen paper. Place the biscuit cutter on the parchment paper and be very careful when you pour the hot mixture into them: keep children and nosey cats out of the way! Spread the mixture as fast as you can, using a knife to push it into the corners, and leave the metal shapes in place until the brittle is completely cool. Have fun!

Time: 30 minutes

100 g/4 oz peeled almonds
100 g/4 oz cane sugar
1 tablespoon freshly squeezed
    lemon juice

1. Toast the almonds and decide if you prefer to keep them whole or chop them up.

2. Get a large sheet of parchment paper ready and fix it to your worktop with tape (this is vital when you're spreading hot caramel).

3. Put the sugar and filtered lemon juice in a pan that will hold almonds. Allow the sugar to dissolve gently over a low heat, moving it just a little with the tip of a spoon. When it is a good caramel colour, take it straight off the heat, add the almonds and mix well.

4. Pour the brittle immediately onto the parchment paper and spread it so that it is 1cm/ 0.3" thick, using a spoon to help you. Leave to cool before breaking it into pieces or gift-wrapping it. It will last a month.

... the sesame and orange version

Sesame brittle needs more sugar than the almond one. This is because sesame seeds are Lilliputian in size and the sugar finds more cracks between them to explore. Spread it out thinly, cut into small pieces and place in mini cake cases. Don't throw away the little splinters from cutting; pop them in a mixer for a few seconds and use them to decorate other sweets.

Time: 30 minutes

100 g/4 oz sesame seeds
200 g/8 oz caster sugar
4-5 tablespoons freshly squeezed
    orange juice

1. Toast the sesame seeds in a large pan. Move them often, and when the seeds start to jump all over the place like crickets having party – pop! pop! pop! (they crackle) – remove immediately from the heat and transfer to a plate to allow them to cool.

2. Continue as for the almond brittle, using orange juice instead of lemon. Spread the brittle out to a thickness of 3 mm/1" (if you're very quick, the caramel – still soft – will pretty much spread out by itself).

recipes

Chocolate and chilli pepper truffles

These are not doses, but a simple ratio between chocolate and cream: five parts one, three the other. The rest is a very personal question of taste, so feel free to experiment, as this is only the basic formula. The lovely thing about chocolate truffles (besides the fact that you eat them) is that you can create so many different versions!

TIME: 1 HOUR

MAKES 35-40 TRUFFLES

200 g/8 oz dark chocolate (70% cocoa)
120 g/just under 6 oz fresh whipping cream
A pinch of salt
1 teaspoon rum
A pinch of chilli pepper (more or less generous, according to your taste)
3 tablespoons bitter cocoa powder

1. Cut the chocolate into the smallest pieces you can (use a knife and be precise; cut tiny regular pieces) and put them in a bowl.

2. Warm the cream in a small pan and turn off the heat as soon as it begins to boil (don't wait for it to start rising; you only have to see large bubbles around the edge of the pan). Pour it in a thin stream onto the chocolate, wait a few seconds then mix with a spoon until it has completely dissolved. At first it will seem too liquid, and there will be a few chocolate pieces that won't dissolve, but have faith; you need a little patience for the chocolate to understand that its ideal partner is cream. Keep mixing vigorously until you get a dense shiny cream. Add the rum and the salt.

3. At this stage, the temptation to dip your finger in the chocolate mixture will be extremely strong and you'll be thinking that (sadly) this is not quite the thing to do in the kitchen. But you are wrong, because to put a finger in the chocolate is exactly what you must do, even two fingers to be precise, if you don't want to lose control of the chilli. So begin with a pinch (a very small pinch), mix and taste; if the chocolate still tastes "only of chocolate", add more chilli and you are hereby authorised to stick your finger in again (but preferably not the same one you used earlier). Try not to overdo it or you may find yourself with chilli truffles with chocolate rather than chocolate truffles with chilli, which is not exactly recommended!

4. Put the bowl in the fridge for 15-20 minutes, until the mixture has the right consistency for handling. Remember that there is an enduring relationship between cream and chocolate, one that lasts for all time; once the ganache solidifies it will not melt, so don't let it get too cool before you use it.

5. Using a spoon to help you, take pieces off and work with your fingertips to make 2 cm/just over ½" diameter balls. The warmth of your hands will melt the chocolate, so dip your hands in cool water (dry them afterwards) and work as quickly as you can. In any case, prepare yourself for having chocolatey hands and resist the temptation... I think we understand each other!

6. Put a few truffles at a time in a small bowl with the cocoa powder and roll them around until they are completely covered. Place them on a plate or in mini cake cases and keep them out of the fridge. They will last a week, if you can resist.

❄ One ganache, so many truffles! A few ideas:

orange and Grand Marnier: use Grand Marnier instead of rum and grated orange zest instead of cocoa powder
almonds/pistachio nuts: use finely chopped toasted almonds and pistachio nuts instead of cocoa powder
hazelnuts: cover a toasted hazelnut with ganache and use cane sugar and toasted hazelnuts mixed in the blender (in equal parts) instead of cocoa powder
walnuts: use coffee instead of rum and cover half a walnut kernel with ganache

recipes

Signorina Beneduce

Signorina Beneduce was at war with the world, and not because the world was at war with her, but because she had declared it herself. She was one of those people who constantly need an enemy for their own self-realisation, and since in times of peace enemies are scarce, she – with an extraordinary innate talent – invented them herself.

The portion of world in her immediate vicinity consisted of her neighbours in the apartment building, who – she said – conspired night and day to ruin the peaceful life she would have led, if only they hadn't existed. The building had been uninhabited for thirty years, with the exception of the flat occupied by an elderly general, a gentleman who was an expert in belligerent people and so had managed to survive her presence across the landing. The others – some due to natural causes, others by choice – had left. "She made them all leave!" bellowed the general, recalling the times when you could count on the supporting troops in times of battle. "Poor Signora Cohen had a nervous breakdown, and Signor Ronchi the architect even had a stroke!" Now, in all honesty, I couldn't tell you if the decimation by natural causes had been assisted in some way by her intervention, but one thing is certain: all transfers by choice were due to one single cause… or rather, multiple "cases" of her initiation.

Signorina Beneduce, who held the most immaculate matrimonial record – or, if you prefer, the title of the world's most irremediable spinster – had two great passions in life: going to morning and evening Mass, and taking others to court. I couldn't say whether there was a close link between the two, but she certainly cultivated them both with equal dedication. If in church she showed off her dramatic genuflexions, hands together in prayer and eyes wide open to the sky, in court she was famous for her serial complaints. In her guise of stalker of the justice system (it would have collapsed within a week if everyone behaved as she had) she would file petitions with the same ease with which normal women go to the hairdresser's. She collected judicial acts as if they were rare vinyl records or stamps, a hobby like any other, because people should be allowed to choose their own hobbies, wouldn't you agree? Her typical day consisted of two walks to church and more or less the same to legal offices (she used several) so when you met her on the stairs she would always have an envelope of documents under her arm and she was in such a hurry because "These lawyers, you have to chase them up, you know! And I jolly well pay them enough, too!"

We did not know much about lawsuits she launched left, right and centre, but we were always made well aware of those concerning condominium life. With the arrival of new owners, the building had undergone a long period of renovation: the façade had been restored to its former glory, and finally new electrical and plumbing systems hade been installed. There was even a lift, which had been positioned in an inside courtyard so as not to spoil the great staircase, and everyone was – with a only few differences of opinion – more or less satisfied. Everyone, except her. And she wasn't even living there at the time.

stories

She had started by suing the builder for the disappearance of the clothes line, and a pulley that – she said – she used to carry up her shopping bags. Well, would you like to try explaining the new lift to her? She didn't want it, and furthermore it was made of glass, and the general might peep at her through her window, on his way up, when she was "en déshabillé".

"I don't even want to see her on the stairs in her coat, let alone her slip!" the general had burst out, omitting the fact that he was approaching eighty, and his eyesight was not what it used to be. Needless to say, a letter from the lawyer arrived in his mailbox, too.

Then it had been the turn of the electrician and the plumber, who were guilty of having left her in the dark and without water: of course, she was never present for their appointments and when she had finally let them in, she had refused to let them work. "They want to demolish my wall!" she had shouted at the administrator, who had rushed to the scene to calm troubled waters.

"It's just a few holes to remove the old wires… please, allow us to install the new systems, so at least we can finish the job…" Nothing to do, she refused to listen. And she had taken him to court, too, because all the suspended work meant that she couldn't live in her own house.

As if all that weren't enough, since water was a right she had commissioned a blitz one early morning, and we had woken up with a huge blue snake fixed to the front of the building, leading from the meter and ending... guess where? After all, water was a right, wasn't it? What else could she do? Until the situation was completely clear, did she also have to pay the bills?

It was the carpenter's turn next: her front door was the only one not to have been restored with the others, because her own trustworthy craftsman was better at the job. One month later, she took him to court, too, followed by the builder who had to fix her interiors, and then two other neighbours.

In this riot of documents, complaints and court summonses, life at the building had become sheer hell. She would turn up at condominium meetings escorted by a lawyer who earned his fees reeling off interminable cahiers de doléances. Two administrators had already succumbed, a third was wavering. We were all exhausted.

The last straw was during the umpteenth meeting (the only one she had ever attended without an escort) with three telephone calls in rapid succession: to traffic wardens, carabinieri and the police. She yelled into the mouthpiece, declaring that her neighbours were holding her hostage in a room located at number x in Whatever Road (by this time she knew how to speak like a lawyer, too) and were preventing her from speaking. Well, taken literally, this would have been a kidnapping attempt, but as the police were highly aware of her excesses no-one arrived to free her.

The following day, the other inhabitants met for a plenary meeting without her knowledge to decide what to do: Signorina Beneduce had lost every lawsuit she had filed, but her excesses caused a huge amount of stress and work anyway.

"She'll never stop! She wants to kill us all. But I won't have a stroke on her account!" shouted the general, the face gone puce and the blood pressure clearly well over the limit.

The lady who lived downstairs, victim of a water leak that could not be fixed because Signorina refused to allow her flat to be inspected, had collapsed into a chair.

The architects on the first floor, who had pleaded for more suitable mailboxes but Signorina threatened to take them to court if the old ones were removed, were completely worn out.

"Maybe we just need to have more patience, make her understand that we can't live like this, perhaps just try to handle her in a different way…" I ventured.

"And what other way would you suggest with that lunatic? Do you want to try?"

"No. I really don't, actually…"

Too late. The peace-keeping mission was approved unanimously. Some weeks later, my husband and I rang the doorbell of Signorina Beneduce's temporary apartment, located at number x in Whatever Road due to the fact that the condominium residents (including ourselves, as well as her) had forced her "de facto", with repeted harassment, to live elsewhere.

A Siberian wind swept down the road, blowing the Christmas lights outside the Town Hall. A few random snowflakes began to fall, people hurried around loaded up with parcels. Celebration was in the air: there were two days left until Christmas.

My husband was furious. "Only you could have thought of doing this! May I remind you that it's our holiday?"

"Exactly. We're devoting some time to the cause: you never know, it might actually work…"

Many times, through the course of that visit, I thought I'd been the victim of my own incurable optimism. The faith in human beings should be dosed with greater economy.

"Signorina" – I said, after hours of lengthy explanations – "it's not exactly much fun going to the lawyers all the time, is it? Until now you've lost all the cases, you have even had to pay damages. I know you're a woman of faith; perhaps all this money could be spent in more charitable ways…"

She looked at me with wild eyes. "Of course it's not much fun! No fun at all. It is a question of civility, my dear lady: we can't always pick up a rifle…"

The general was right: that woman was an eternally belligerent human being, like one of those Japanese soldiers hidden in the jungle for decades, who had never resigned themselves to the end of the war. According to her logic, taking people to court was the only alternative to a gunshot, an act of supreme civility in the Far West of life, even though it merely concerned deciding which varnish to put on the front door or the colour of the mailboxes.

It was time to say goodbye when I remembered the parcel in my bag: some chocolate truffles I'd made for my mother-in-law. No premeditation, just flash of inspiration: after all, wasn't the whole situation pretty surreal? It was surely worth attempting to do the complete opposite of what she expected.

"Signorina, I almost forgot: I made these for you. I hope you like chocolate…"

Her face lit up before she could realise it. In such cases kindness is very fast acting, the dynamic is unstoppable, there isn't even time for you to call the lawyer. It was too late for her to change expression. I made the most of it and smiled.

She murmured an embarrassed "Thank you, but… why?"

"Because it's Christmas!" I declared, and smiled again.

In Signorina Beneduce's iron logic, a gift could never just be a gift: it had to hide some kind of request or ulterior motive. In her culture, to accept a gift was the same as to bury the hatchet.

She was trapped.

"And what can I give you in return?" she groaned in dismay, as if speaking to herself.

"Nothing! Just smile…"

She did her best, I'll admit, even if the result was no more than a scribble drawn on the serrated lips of her dry wizened face. But she wouldn't let us leave without putting some oranges from her garden in a bag and… she even wished us a Happy Christmas!

"She'll have put rat poison in those…" said my husband as he went out of the door.

"Oh come on, you're getting just like the old general! We need to put an end to this story, you know"

The Town Hall lights had stopped swaying, even the wind had resigned itself to being better behaved: there were only two days left until Christmas.

Signorina Beneduce reappeared on the stairs of our building shortly after New Year. "They were delicious, your chocolates. Did you really make them yourself?" Then she adjusted her coat collar, looked around, almost ashamed of what she took to be a weakness, and added: "I thought I'd sort out the front door, I just need to know which wax I should use…"

Suddenly a light went on, just for me, and started flashing a great "Wow!"

At that moment, the general came out of his flat. "What have you done to her?!?" he whispered in disbelief.

"I didn't do a thing; it was all down to Christmas…"

"Let's hope it lasts all year. Goodbye Signora!" And with a slight bow he disappeared through the lift doors.

Since in the universe nothing is created and nothing is destroyed, I wonder where on earth all Signorina Beneduce's spinster malevolence had disappeared to? It must have reincarnated itself into something different, but it didn't enter anyone's head to go and look for it.

The mailboxes went up only two years later, but shortly afterwards the plumber was finally able to get into her flat and finish his work. The lady on the first floor got her bathroom working again, after months of waiting. Mirrors were added to the inside walls of the lift, so there was no possibility for anyone to peep into the front windows on its journey: at first the general kept bumping his head trying to go out the wrong way, but with the help of new lenses he finally managed to walk through the right door. The electrician never managed to put up the new entry phone system, but she came to a settlement with the carpenter. One case concluded swiftly, two others carried on for years (of course the condominium won in the end) but no others were initiated. Signorina Beneduce continued to visit lawyers and courts (because people should be allowed to choose their own hobbies, wouldn't you agree?), but her darts disguised as judicial acts never came through that front door again. She gave up being escorted by a lawyer, and my husband was the only person to make her see sense when necessary.

Every time she met me on the stairs, she made a huge effort to smile, but she was forced to: for years I kept sending her a small box of chocolate truffles every Christmas.

Knäck: the Swedish toffee for absolute beginners

*You need sugar, cream and golden syrup in equal measure for this fast and easy-to-prepare toffee.
This recipe is borrowed from the Swedish tradition, but I guarantee that it will work everywhere; if you follow the
instructions there's no reason why you shouldn't succeed! Just like some DIY kit furniture…*

Time: 1 hour

Makes 30 pieces

100 g/4 oz caster sugar
100 ml/3 ½ fl oz fresh whipping
   cream
100 ml/3 ½ fl oz golden syrup
1 teaspoon cold butter
Chopped toasted almonds

1. Prepare a tray with 30 mini cake cases. Place them side by side so that they can't go for a stroll wherever they like, but not too close otherwise your knäck will come out wonky.

2. Put the sugar, cream and golden syrup in a small pan. A steel heavy-based pan is better (between you and me, a non-stick pan is fine, but make sure it isn't the one you use for frying sardines or making garlic sauce).

3. Bring to the boil on the smallest hob ring, keep mixing with a wooden spoon (the same rules apply as for the pan), then turn the heat down to its lowest setting (or even lower, if you can).
In fifteen minutes time you need to start testing the consistency of the mixture. At that time, the mixture will appear frothy: a lot of foam will boil up, that's fine, but mix it from time to time. Between one mix and another, prepare a bowl of cold water and keep it near to hand.

4. After 15 minutes boiling time (kept at the lowest heat possible) start testing the consistency of the knäck. Let a large blob of it drop from the spoon into the bowl with the cold water and watch what happens: your goal is to manage to press the drops between two fingers and make a pliable ball with the consistency of plasticine (I hope you played with plasticine when you were small, because I can't think of any other comparison).
Plan to make more than one attempt, and don't leave too much time between one attempt and another; one minute can make all the difference and if you cook it too much, the knäck becomes hard. When the "plasticine ball attempt"(basic definition, but it helps to get the idea across) gives the expected result, turn off the hob, add the butter and mix until every last bubble has disappeared.

5. Quickly pour the mixture into the mini cake cases, filling each one to ¾ of its capacity (use a spoon). Work rapidly because it hardens fast, but be careful, concentrate hard and be precise. Try to avoid any distractions because hot caramel burns unforgivingly, so park your four-legged friends on the terrace and keep your children occupied in other activities.

6. You can call the children back when the mini cake cases are full: sprinkling the knäck with almonds is fun and danger-free! The only risk is that, once your knäck has reached an acceptable temperature, a few mini cake cases will be emptied before you've even had time to show them off on your cake stand…

❄ *If you're not sure whether your mini cake cases are perfectly non-stick (it happens…), dip a brush in a tiny bit of sunflower oil, eliminating any excess with kitchen paper, and brush inside every mini cake case.*

recipes

Walnut and almond nougat

You need a little patience and a partner-in-crime to make nougat. The technique is simple, but you should take care in certain steps and be well-organised. The only difficulty is to identify the moment in which the honey and sugar are at the right temperature to be added to the egg white; you can do it without a thermometer (I have never had one myself). As far as technological equipment is concerned, the only thing you really need is an electric beater with whisks and hooks. Get yourself a couple of significantly heavy volumes (heavy in the physical sense, not metaphorical); you'll need them to press the nougat to perfection. Tomes of encyclopedias and dictionaries are ideal: my beloved old Latin dictionary has been given a new lease of life in my kitchen since I started making nougat…

TIME: 1½ HOURS

FOR THE NOUGAT
150 g/6 oz peeled almonds
50 g/2 oz walnut pieces
200 g/8 oz clear runny honey
     (such as acacia, wildflower,
     orange blossom)
50 g/2 oz glucose syrup
200 g/8 oz caster sugar
50 ml/1½ fl oz water
1 egg white

FOR THE FINISHING
100 g/4 oz dark chocolate
     (70% cocoa)

1. Toast the nuts

Toast the walnuts and almonds, put them in a large-mesh sieve, and shake them to eliminate the skins and dark bits that would otherwise spoil your nougat. Leave to cool and break up the walnuts with your hands (each one into 2-3 pieces). Cut the almonds in half with a knife (not all, just about a third).

Time for a methodological pause – From now on you'll read several things that seem minor, even just plain crazy, but it's best to be well-organised during this stage so as not to find yourself in trouble towards the end, when the rhythm accelerates and every single move you make requires surgical precision (ok, let's not exaggerate: the worst you would do is murder your nougat, which in any case would still be edible, but just to get my message across).

For example, glucose and honey need to be measured accurately, so put the pans you'll be using for cooking them on the weighing scales, adjust the scales, then place the ingredients directly in the pans on the scales (so you won't even lose a single ounce). It would be preferable for these pans to have a heavy base and – essential! – a long handle, because you need to pour a stream of hot liquid onto a meringue as you whip it.

2. Prepare all the ingredients…

So, as I said, measure the honey into small pan no. 1.

Put the following ingredients into small pan no. 2, in this exact order: the glucose, the sugar and water, without mixing. Have the toasted nuts at hand.

Break the egg and separate the white (without a minimal trace of yolk, otherwise you can forget whipping it) and put it in a very large bowl (preferably metal or ceramic). Beat the white gently; it should be frothy but still soft. Put the bowl on a worktop free of clutter and where there is enough space for two people to work together.

… and the utensils

Position the electric beater near the bowl: attach the whisks (you'll be using these first) and keep the hooks nearby for the nougat mixture (you'll be using these next).
Cut two sheets of parchment paper of about 30 x 40cm/12" x 15 ½" and fix one of them to the worktop with sellotape (you'll realise why when it comes to spreading out the nougat). Have a rolling pin to hand. Finally, find yourself a trusty accomplice who is able to pour a hot stream of honey and sugar while you use the whisks in the bowl,

(so, not a child) and explain what you are going to do together. And now... let the fun begin!

3. **Dissolve the honey and sugar**

Put both the small pans over the heat: choose the smallest hob rings and adjust the heat to a moderate level (if you don't have two hob rings of the same size, make sure that the bigger one is at minimum heat and the smaller a little higher; you need to have the honey and sugar at the right temperature more or less at the same time).

This will take about 15 minutes, so prepare two bowls of cold water nearby and two teaspoons: you'll need these to test when the sugars are ready, in the following way:

Honey: mix only from time to time, it shouldn't brown too much. After 8-10 minutes take a small amount with a spoon and pour it in the water: if you manage to make a soft ball with it between two fingers, it's ready. If it slides between your fingers, carry on cooking and try again after 1-2 minutes (try more than once if necessary).

Sugar: mix only now and again, without getting it on the edges of the pan (otherwise crystals begin to form which turn into lumps in the nougat). After 8-10 minutes take a small quantity with the teaspoon and pour it into the water: you should be able to form a small soft ball between two fingers, but when you lengthen it by pulling with both hands in opposite directions, the threads that form should break and not be elastic and lengthen continuously. If this doesn't happen at the first attempt, carry on cooking and try again after 1-2 minutes (try further attempts as necessary).

4. **Add the honey first and then the sugar to the egg white**

When the honey is ready, ask your helper to pour it in a stream into the bowl, while you whip up the egg white with the whisks at low speed. You'll see the mixture swell and become glossy within a minute or two; the aroma is divine. The pouring shouldn't be too slow, otherwise the honey will cool in the pan and stick to it. Use a spoon to help you, but remember that the honey will quickly harden, so be prepared to leave a little of it (in other words, you'll never manage to completely empty your pans). Once you have used up all the honey, do the same thing with the sugar, whisking continuously.

The two pouring sessions shouldn't take more than a few minutes altogether, given the quantities. If, while you're working with the honey, the sugar remains in the pan off the heat, nothing will happen (as long as you don't leave it for a quarter of an hour).

5. **Work the meringue until it is cool**

By now you should have a pan full of glossy meringue: firm, aromatic and quite hot. Replace the whisks with the hooks (a little mixture will stick but you'll have to leave it there) and continue to work for 3-5 minutes, until you feel the temperature of the bowl goes from hot to just a little more than warm. This stage is fundamental, if you don't wish your nougat to be excessively soft. As the mixture will gradually harden, ask your helper to keep the bowl steady while you work. Don't be too relaxed about the timing here, otherwise you won't manage to add the nuts and spread the mixture out.

6. **Add the nuts**

Forget the electric beater and add the almonds and walnuts all in one go; mix firmly and rapidly with a spoon to combine everything well.

7. **Spread out the nougat with a rolling pin**

Pour the mixture onto the parchment paper immediately, spread it out with a spoon (it will be very hard), put the other sheet of parchment paper on the top and press the mixture down with the rolling pin to 1 ½ cm/½". Be as quick as you can! Turn it and work it from the other side as well, to ensure it is perfectly even.

8. **A night with a dictionary and then... chocolate!**

Leave the nougat to dry in a cool place (but not the fridge), preferably weighted down; a couple of old books such as dictionaries are ideal.

The next day, remove the parchment paper carefully from the top. Melt the chocolate in a bain-marie, warm it gently and then pour it on top of the nougat. Spread it out with the back of a spoon and leave the nougat to dry for a few hours before you finally relish it.

Festive
cheerful snacks

A wreath of crackers for Monsieur Camembert

This is a funny idea for serving cheese and chutney. Cut stars of different sizes and casually overlap them. If you can, make a shooting star shape, too (have you ever had Christmas without a shooting star?). Buy a camembert cheese in a stapled wooden box without glue, if you don't want the glue and cheese to go on the table inextricably mixed. Bring it to the table boiling hot with an extra bowl of crackers because your wreath will disappear rapidly! The first to find the shooting star can make a wish…

TIME: 1½ HOURS (EXCLUDING TIME FOR MELTING THE CAMEMBERT)

MAKES 2 WREATHS 25 CM/JUST UNDER 10" IN DIAMETER OR 1 WREATH + A BOWLFUL OF CRACKERS

FOR THE DOUGH
150 g/6 oz whole-weat flour
100 g/4 oz whole-weat oat flour
2 tablespoons cumin seeds
1 tablespoon cane sugar
1 teaspoon salt
130ml/4 ½ fl oz water
50ml/1 ½ fl oz extra-virgin olive oil

FOR THE FINISHING
1 egg white
Salt
1 tablespoon cane sugar
1 tablespoon cumin seeds

1. Preheat the oven to 200°C/400°F. Line a baking tray with parchment paper and draw round the circumference of the camembert box with a pencil.

2. Put the flours, cumin seeds, sugar and salt into a bowl. Mix thoroughly and make a well in the centre.

3. Put the water and oil in a jug and mix. Pour the mixture into the bowl of dry ingredients and mix with a spoon until the dough begins to come together (don't worry if it doesn't quite make a homogenous ball). Leave to rest for 10-15 minutes with a plate to cover it so that it doesn't dry out.

4. Work the dough quickly with your hands in the bowl until it comes together, then transfer to the worktop and work it again for another minute (no more if you want your crackers to be fragrant). Flour the worktop and spread the dough out with a rolling pin to one sheet of 2 mm/just under 1" thick (you don't need to get your ruler, just roll it out as thin as it will go…).

5. Cut the crackers out and place them on the baking tray around the pencil line, overlapping without pressing down too much. Beat the egg white with 2 tablespoons water and quickly brush the wreath; sprinkle with the salt, sugar and cumin. Pop it in the oven. Keep the remaining crackers on the worktop to be baked afterwards.

6. Bake for 15-20 minutes until it is golden brown. Leave to cool before transferring to a plate; the wreath is very fragile as soon as it is cooked, so lift it with the parchment paper. Bake the remaining crackers (or your second wreath).

7. When it's time to serve the camembert, take it out of its box, unwrap it, make a few cuts in the top, place it back in the box and wrap some string around it to prevent it from opening while cooking. Put it in a preheated oven (about 200°C/400°F) on a heat-resistant plate. Don't worry if a little cheese drips from the bottom, this often happens! You'll know it's ready when it begins to seep through the cuts. Wear your oven mitts when you take it out of the oven, and resist the urge to dip a finger in… it's like molten lava! Place it in its box in the middle of the wreath and serve immediately.

❄ *The cracker dough is a bit hard to knead, because you need to roll it out thinly and cut it precisely. If your flours are very dry (this happens, especially when wholemeal) you'll notice when you start to work that it's difficult for the dough to come together. If this is the case, add a few spoons of water. Try to make the best of your cutters to reduce the amount of residual dough and avoid kneading it again. Playing around with cutters of different sizes makes things easier. If you end up with any blunt star, you can always cover it up with a perfectly shaped one…*

recipes

Seeded rye crackers

Leave these to cool completely before trying them: they need to lose every trace of moisture to be presented on cracking form for their appointment with their plate of cheese, vegetable dip or chutney! Or even with that lonely glass of wine; when coupled with a forest of crunchy Christmas trees for company you'll have quite an aperitif! The little trees will disappear one crunch after another, to the joy of your friends. You can always promise them you'll plan to create another forest with your trusty rolling pin very soon...

TIME: 1 HOUR 45 MINUTES
(FOR 2 OR 3 BATCHES)

MAKES 25 LARGE TREES AND 50 SMALL ONES (WITH MY CUTTERS THAT MEASURE 7.5 X 9 CM/3" X 3 ½" AND 4.5 X 6.5 CM/JUST OVER 1 ½" X 2 ½")

FOR THE DOUGH
150 g/6 oz all-purpose flour
100 g/4 oz wholemeal rye flour
100 g/4 oz mix of sesame, flax, pumpkin and sunflower seeds
1 teaspoon cane sugar
1 teaspoon salt
½ teaspoon bicarbonate of soda
140 ml/4 ½ fl oz water
60 ml/2 fl oz extra-virgin olive oil

FOR THE FINISHING
1 egg white
table salt
2 tablespoons seed mix

1. Preheat the oven to 200°C/400°F and line a baking tray with parchment paper.

2. Put the flours, seeds, sugar, salt and the sieved bicarbonate of soda into a bowl. Mix thoroughly and make a well in the centre.

3. Mix the oil and water in a jug, pour onto the dry ingredients in the bowl and mix with a spoon until the dough comes together in one ball. It will seem sticky and impossible to work with your hands but don't add more flour; the rye will absorb any moisture, you just have to give it a little time. Work the dough with your hands for one minute; stop as soon as the dough becomes homogenous.

4. Divide it into two parts. Leave one under the upturned bowl and roll the other out as much as you can (the limit is the same as the thickness of the pumpkin seeds, the chubbiest of all your ingredients). A piece of advice: lightly flour your worktop, hands and rolling pin.

5. Cut the crackers into whatever shapes you prefer, and place them on the baking tray (they don't expand on cooking so they can stay next to each other without arguing). When the first batch is ready to bake, pop it in the fridge for 10 minutes without covering (making sure that you place it as far away as possible from fishy foods and other strong aromas...).

6. Remove the tray from the fridge and brush quickly with the egg white (which you have just beaten with 2 spoonfuls of water). Sprinkle with the salt and seeds, then bake for 15-20 minutes, turning halfway through the cooking time.

❄ *These crackers will keep for over a month, if you manage to make them last that long! The ideal container is a tin box, but you must make sure the crackers are completely cool before putting them in the box; there mustn't be any trace of moisture in order to avoid damage. Alternatively you could keep them in a glass jar, one of those with a loose lid (or even without a lid if you can find a protected place for them). If you live in one of those flats in the city with the heating on full blast (where there's always a lady on the top floor who feels that General Winter has arrived and the whole condominium should prepare itself to confront a Siberian Freeze as soon as it starts getting a little chilly), the crackers will gradually dry out and become even crunchier.*

If, however, you live near a rainforest or in an old watermill and the humidity levels in your kitchen resemble those of a Turkish bath, no tin on earth will be good enough but you'll have a great excuse to eat them as soon as possible!

recipes

Irina's Granny's kefir blinis

The Irina in question is still the same, the Soviet pancakes' one from my book "Fragole a merenda", who measures sugar and flour in Stalin's glasses and hands me some of her grandmother's recipes, vintage ones of before the fall of the Berlin Wall. The mainstay of our family organisation, Irina is my accomplice in most of my culinary adventures, and she joins in enthusiastically with even the hardest of tasks: if it weren't for her, just to say, my torrone production would be significantly reduced… She has honey and rose jam sent from home, and even hens and "Stalin's glasses" whenever needed – I've got one, too, as I need it for translating her recipes. She makes incredibly soft and light blinis, that couldn't be further away from the vacuum-packed shrivelled-up pancakes sold in shops as "blinis"… Irina's Granny's doses are generous, but you can easily half them. All that remains is for you to get hold of some kefir and try. They sell it in organic food shops, chic expensive delicatessens, and certain shops – anything but chic – of cheap products for an immigrant, extremely exclusive clientele. It's from one of these that Irina brings me the most exquisite kefir that I have ever tasted. As for blinis, the Soviet rule states that they should be accompanied by a little sour cream, before you decide whether to prepare the sweet or the savoury version. Blinis and sour cream together are like my grandparents: a unique, inseparable and enviable couple. So, whether you choose salmon or red berries, it doesn't matter: you'll love your blinis anyway. If, however, you're completely undecided, go for a compromise and try honey and gorgonzola: a perfect balance. Ok, it's not exactly sour cream, but it really works!

TIME: 1 HOUR

MAKES 50 BLINIS OF ABOUT 6 CM/2"

500 ml/17 fl oz kefir
2 large eggs
2 teaspoons caster sugar
4 pinches of salt
200 g/8 oz all-purpose flour
1 level teaspoon bicarbonate of soda
A knob of butter for the frying pan

1. Put the kefir, eggs, sugar and salt into a bowl. Whisk to mix well.

2. Add the flour all at once, and whisk vigorously until the mixture becomes a smooth batter completely free of lumps.

3. Finally, add the sieved bicarbonate of soda and mix, but this time without beating; limit yourself to circular movements and avoid lifting the whisk (please don't ask me why because I have no idea, but I have learned to follow Irina's Granny's directions to the letter: they always make sense even when I may not realise it).

4. Warm a non-stick frying pan, drop the knob of butter in with a fork and spread it round the pan at the speed of light (you only need a thin layer). When it is hot, drop in a ladleful of batter for each blini. You can choose the size; if I have decided to make them savoury, I make small ones, 6 cm/2" in diameter, otherwise they look like pancakes. One thing you must ensure, however, is the shape: they must be perfectly round, so be sure to keep the batter away from the edges of the pan, so that it expands in a regular concentric way.

5. Let them cook for a couple of minutes each side. Keep an eye on the surface of your blinis: when the bubbles begin to pop and become little holes, it's time to turn them over… a scientifically proven Soviet test! As Irina says… Between one batch and another, clean the pan with kitchen paper if there is any residue, but don't add any more butter if you want your blinis to come out without being scorched black around the edges.

6. Eat them hot (as I prefer them) or cold (as Irina's Granny likes them). And if they run out… just make some more!

A goose, chicken and foie gras story

I'm an unrepentant omnivore. I eat everything out of curiosity even more so than flavour, and I don't resign myself to those awful Taliban-style limitations that are all the rage now – six months one ban, six months another, and in the six months later yet another – and that would turn us into eaters of lactose-free dairy products, gluten-free carbohydrates, sugar-free desserts, and butter… for pity's sake, don't you know that saying its very name is enough to kill you? In these dark times populated by fanatics and penitents of all kinds, I strive to maintain my equilibrium with these relentlessly growing prohibitions: the culinary penal code is chock-full of frightening, reprehensible crimes, punished by improvised and relentless people's tribunals.

I have a friend who, when she bumps into me eating a lovely ham croissant at the pastry shop round the corner (and I can assure you they make gorgeous ones!) is more than capable of looking down at me as if I was in my pyjamas with messy hair at a theatre premiere. She drinks certain herbal teas in sachets that are distinctly horrifying (even the poor barista is horrified, while he prepares them), and while she lists all the poisons contained in my cappuccino (stuff that would knock you dead in an instant, if even a cent of what she says was true), I always wonder what she would say if she saw me go into the butcher's over the road: a place of perdition, a spiritual abyss, a black hole of the soul for beings who are in perfect harmony with the universe, like her.

I would never tell her that I am the elderly butcher's favourite. He and I have long chats – away from prying ears, given the unfavourable conjuncture – about some cuts of meat that no-one wants anymore, and how a string of sausages has by now become more alarming than a hoard of Barbarians on the horizon. He's the one who gets small chicken livers for me to make into pâté; he hands over the package with a conspiratorial grin as if to say: "We understand each other, you and I…" and then asks me to explain in front of everyone what I am going to do. I believe he truly enjoys it. He smiles while I describe the smell of thyme and bay, and how chicken liver pâté – on a slice of toasted black bread, with a glass of Sauternes – has become part of my Christmas (and I don't like liver…).

"So you are in favour of torturing geese?" a fanatic reproached me one day, staring at me as if I was a ruthless serial killer.

I usually have an answer ready, almost too ready, and I have to summon all my self-control to stop it escaping. That time it was easy… a monosyllable beginning with "y".

It was my friend the butcher who stepped in, with all the politeness he reserves for his customers, and with some concern for the neat pile of foie-gras jars towering on the highest shelf of the shop.

"I can tell you, madam, that the livers this lady has are chicken livers, and I can assure you that the chickens I buy have a better life than… live as well as your dog!" and he threw a meatball over the counter, in the direction of a droopy four-legged creature dressed in a trendy dog jacket.

A desperate cry broke through the tranquil hum of the shop. "For heaven's sake! No meat! He's got a skin problem and the vet told me to feed him on nothing but fennels, for a few days…"

"And does he eat them?!?" asked the poor butcher, in total disbelief.

"With some difficulty, but he knows it's for his own good… isn't that right, my darling?" and they began to smooch each other mouth to mouth (well, mouth to beak).

Life in the shop carried on as usual, it was quiet at that hour: the clicking of the till, the foil packages ready to be delivered, the shutter already half lowered.

"Do you really think that vets prescribe fennels to dogs, these days?" he asked me, eyes widening in astonishment, as soon as the six-legged duo had closed the door behind them.

"Who knows…? But you mustn't ask me such questions, when you know certain people are around!"

We laughed like two old partners-in-crime, which is what we really are, by now (don't tell my friend, please).

Once back home, I couldn't stop thinking about him while thyme and bay were making friends with garlic and shallots in my frying pan, sliding about together on a layer of butter. A delicious smell wafted around the kitchen.

Two bottles of Sauternes winked at me from the shelf above my head. The lead grey sky carried a sign saying "snow!" It would be a freezing, fantastic Christmas…

Liver pâté with port wine

This is delicious on a freshly toasted slice of sapa bread and when accompanied by chutney it becomes positively fantastic. Quality is fundamental; get yourself the best livers you can find from chickens who have had a good life, and honour them… I always have a bottle of port at home for a touch of "spirit" and it goes very well in this recipe, but feel free to experiment: after all, that's the beauty of cooking… and of Christmas!

TIME: 1 HOUR

MAKES A 400 ML/13 ½ FL OZ JAR

300 g/12 oz chicken livers
2 eggs
100 g/4 oz soft butter
1 clove garlic, skin on
50 g/2 oz shallots
5 twigs fresh thyme
2-3 fresh bay leaves
5 juniper berries
1 tablespoon cane sugar
table salt
freshly milled black pepper
1 small 50 ml/1 ½ fl oz glass
  of port
½ cube gelatine

1. Take out the butter from the fridge beforehand because it needs to be soft. Rinse the chicken livers under running water, remove all trace of filaments and make sure there are no pieces of other offal. Leave to drain in a colander.

2. Hard-boil the eggs. The yolk needs to be well done but don't let it turn green. Keep them in cold water for a little while, then shell them and remove the yolks.

3. Peel and rinse the shallots, rinse the thyme and bay leaves. Put a third of the butter into a non-stick frying pan and add the crushed garlic clove, the thinly sliced shallots, thyme, bay leaves and juniper. Stir from time to time and when the shallots have become transparent, add the cane sugar and let them caramelise for one or two minutes, stirring. Remove the vegetables from the pan, keeping as much of the seasoned butter in the pan as you do so, and put the vegetables to one side (throw away the garlic).

4. Put the chicken livers in the pan whole (this is important, otherwise it would be difficult to cook them evenly). Let them cook in the butter; press them lightly with a wooden spoon if you see parts of them fold up a little, otherwise the edges may end up raw. Add salt and pepper, turn them and continue cooking on the other side. Cook them for no more than 5-8 minutes in total; the livers must be cooked on the outside but still pink inside, so check one with the tip of a knife before you turn off the heat. If, like me, you are not keen on rare meat, the exact colour should be beige-rose, but be careful because half a minute can make all the difference… and overcooked chicken livers lose their soft creaminess.

5. Remove them from the pan. Add the port to the cooking juices (a professional cook would say: "Deglaze the pan with the port"), allow the alcohol to evaporate (a minute is enough) and then remove from the heat.

6. Put the caramelised vegetables (remove only the juniper and bay leaves, keeping the thyme, taking the leaves off the stem) into the container of a hand blender. Add the crumbled egg yolk, chicken livers, and all the cooking juices – make sure you save every last precious drop from the pan. Work with the blender (you may need to use just half the quantity of livers at first, to reduce the volume) and then add the butter, which by now will be soft. Work the mixture until it becomes a cream without a trace of lumps.

7. Transfer the pâté to a glass (or ceramic) super-clean container, eliminate any bubbles with a knife or a teaspoon, smooth the surface and put it in the fridge. When it is completely cool, prepare the gelatine following packet instructions, leave to cool and then pour it over the pâté to a thickness of a few millimetres (not even ¼"), to make sure it is well sealed.

Your chicken liver pâté keeps well in the fridge for about a week. If you wish to gift it, avoid making it travel of the fridge: it is extremely delicate and won't keep more than a few hours.

❄ *If you don't manage to eliminate all the lumps with your hand blender, you could pass the pâté through a sieve, using a spoon to help you. I never do this, but you should know that it does work; you just need a lot of patience.*

recipes

anacardi al
miele e curry

Nuts in honey and salt

You can become easily addicted; I think it's only right to inform you before you start getting all the ingredients ready. They're easy to make, everyone loves them, they're great for buffets and are extremely satisfying on their own or as an aperitif snack. As with all simple recipes, quality of the ingredients is fundamental, so get the best nuts you can. I'm saying this because, every now and again, I find a distinctly rancid smell when someone opens certain dubious packets right under my nose. Nuts are always on tempting display in supermarkets, they seem cheap but if you check the weight, you'll discover they are not. So avoid these tiny packets like the plague. Find a well-stocked grocery store, a passionate greengrocer or a supermarket with trustworthy suppliers (they do exist) and if possible, taste before you buy: almonds and hazelnuts are not all the same, just like the people who sell them. As far as salt is concerned, I don't get all excited about those extravagant types from the other side of the world, but I do use Camargue fleur de sel for these recipes: it is delicate and has smaller crystals than ordinary cooking salt. Of course, it's more expensive than the salt you use for your pasta cooking water… but you don't have to use it to salt your pasta water!
If you use large crystal cooking salt, instead, do not exaggerate, especially if the crystals are very big.

Hazelnuts coated in honey and salt

Time: 10 minutes if you use ready toasted hazelnuts, 40 minutes if you have to toast them yourself (this is valid for other recipes that follow)

100 g/4 oz peeled hazelnuts
2 tablespoons honey
fleur de sel

1. Toast the hazelnuts in an oven you have preheated to 180°C/350°F, for about 10 minutes. They should be just golden with a hazelnut aroma (I know, it seems like tautology, but that's the way it is). Allow to cool before proceeding.

2. Melt the honey in a non-stick pan and then throw in the hazelnuts. Stir them around in the honey several times, mixing with a wooden spoon. When the honey has caramelised and begins to darken, remove from the heat (be careful here: it only takes a few seconds of distraction for the honey to blacken).

3. Transfer the hazelnuts to a plate, spread them out and sprinkle with salt without mixing or going over the top with the salt quantity…

Almonds coated in honey and mustard seeds

100 g/4 oz peeled almonds
2 tablespoons honey
1 tablespoon mustard seeds
A pinch of chilli pepper
Fleur de sel

Proceed as for the hazelnuts. At point n. 3, sprinkle the almonds with mustard seeds, chilli pepper and salt.

Cashew nuts coated in honey and curry

100 g/4 oz cashew nuts
2 tablespoons honey
½ teaspoon curry powder
Fleur de sel

Proceed as for the hazelnuts. At point n. 2, add the curry powder to the melted honey in a pan, just before you throw in the cashew nuts.

recipes

nocciole al
miele e sale

chutney di fichi e fichi alla senape

chutney di scalogni e mele

chutney di radicchio all'arancia

chutney di indivia e mandarini

Chutney parade!

Chutney is one of those extraordinary recipes that never fails to work. It is a proportion of variable geometry between ingredients, or rather ingredient categories. In order of appearance: a vinegar and sugar base, a fresh fruit element and one of vegetable origin (among which a nourishing representative of the "onion, shallot, leek and suchlike" family must be included), a dried fruit element, plus aromatic herbs and spices. Chutney has no need of any type of fat (chutney is a jam, after all), but a final drop of alcohol is indispensable. Whatever you have to hand is fine, but you must absolutely include a "spirited" element because the chutney needs it. "Some sort of spirit" as Brenda always said. If you want to dedicate yourself to the admirable art of chutney-making, Christmas is by far the best time to do it: time to relax and lots of friends to test your experiments! As with all art forms, chutney-making requires a minimum of technical knowledge. No problem, I'll give you a hand. The golden rule of proportions is this: 1-2-6: one part sugar, two parts vinegar, six parts fruit and vegetables. More or less, because from now on you will be entering the reign of pure creativity: and you are the artist...

Chutney in 10 steps

1. Mix the vinegar and sugar in a non-stick pan.
2. Add the pieces of fruit as they are ready (to enhance the flavours).
3. Add all the other ingredients without mixing.
4. Turn the heat on only when the pan is complete.
5. Let the contents cook uncovered, mixing so that they do not stick, until all the initial liquid has gone.
6. Only add water if and when it's needed, a little at a time; the chutney must cook in the dense aromatic syrup that has been created, and not float (it works just like a risotto, which is much nicer than boiled rice).
7. You'll know it's ready when you pass the spoon over the bottom of the pan and the space it leaves doesn't close up.
8. Pour the boiling chutney into a spotlessly clean glass jar, eliminating any air bubbles.
9. Keep in the fridge (lid or cling film compulsory); it will last a month and maybe longer.
10. Use it as an accompaniment to mature cheeses and dried fruit, liver pâté, *bollito* (see p. 88) and roasted meats. Above all, do make it! And have fun choosing different ingredients...

recipes

Apple and shallot chutney

TIME: 1 HOUR 15 MINUTES

150 ml/5 fl oz balsamic vinegar
80 g/just over 3 oz muscovado sugar
300 g/12 oz apples
200 g/8 oz shallots
3 knobs fresh ginger
50 g/2 oz dried prunes
50 g/2 oz sultanas
4 cloves
1 tablespoon honey
Table salt
1 small glass grappa or other dry
  liqueur (50 ml/1 ½ fl oz)

(the quantities of fruit and
vegetables are to be considered
without peelings)

1. Quickly rinse the sultanas and soak them in warm water.

2. Put the vinegar and sugar in a wide non-stick frying pan. Add the following, as they are ready:
   - the peeled, chopped and finely sliced apples
   - the peeled, washed and sliced shallots and ginger
   - the dried prunes, each one cut into 4-5 pieces.

3. Add the squeezed out sultanas, cloves, honey and salt (do not exaggerate).

4. Cook uncovered over a medium heat, stir often with a wooden spoon and don't add more liquids: at first the vinegar and the shallot and apple juices will be enough. When the cooking liquid has become syrupy and the mixture risks sticking, add a little water at a time and only when necessary; the chutney mustn't float.

5. Cook for about 30 minutes from boiling time: the apples should not become mushy. When the chutney is ready, add the grappa and let evaporate for a minute before taking off the heat.

6. Pour the boiling chutney into a spotlessly clean glass jar, eliminate any air bubbles with a knife or a spoon and allow to cool before closing the jar. Keep it in the fridge, it will last a month.

Radicchio and orange chutney

TIME: 1 HOUR 15 MINUTES

150 ml/5 fl oz balsamic vinegar
150 g/6 oz whole cane sugar
150 g/6 oz green apples (1-2 apples)
300 g/12 oz radicchio
100 g/4 oz shallots
200 g/8 oz knife-peeled oranges
  (2-3 oranges)
50 g/2 oz dried blueberries
1 teaspoon four spices mix
Table salt
1 small glass (50ml/1 ½ fl oz)
  grappa or other dry liqueur

(the quantities of fruit and
vegetables are to be considered
without peelings)

1. Quickly rinse the blueberries and soak them in warm water.

2. Put the vinegar and sugar in a wide non-stick frying pan. Add the following, as they are ready:
   - the peeled, washed, quartered then finely sliced apples
   - the peeled, washed and finely sliced radicchio and shallots
   - the oranges which you have sliced over a bowl to catch all the juice.

3. Add the squeezed out blueberries, the four spices mix and the salt (do not exaggerate).

4. Cook uncovered over a medium heat, stir often with a wooden spoon and don't add more liquids; at first the vinegar and the fruit and vegetable juices will be enough. When the cooking liquid has become syrupy and the mixture risks sticking, add a little water at a time and only if necessary; the chutney mustn't float.

5. Cook for about 40 minutes from boiling time. When the chutney is ready, add the grappa and let evaporate for a minute before taking off the heat.

6. Pour the boiling chutney into a spotlessly clean glass jar, eliminate any air bubbles with a knife or a spoon and allow to cool before closing the jar. Keep it in the fridge, it will last a month.

recipes

Pear, fig and mustard chutney

TIME: 1 HOUR 15 MINUTES

200 ml/just over 6 ½ fl oz cider
    vinegar
100 g/4 oz cane sugar
350 g/14 oz pears
200 g/8 oz red onions
1 clove garlic
2 bay leaves
5 juniper berries
1 tablespoon mustard seeds
1 tablespoon honey
Table salt
1 teaspoon mustard powder
80 g/just over 3 oz soft dried figs
1 small glass (50ml/1 ½ fl oz)
    cognac or other dry liqueur

(the quantities of fruit and
vegetables are to be considered
without peelings)

1. Put the vinegar and sugar in a wide non-stick frying pan. Add the following, as they are ready:
- the peeled, washed, quartered and then finely sliced pears
- the peeled, washed and finely sliced onions and garlic (remove the green part of the garlic if present)
- the rinsed bay leaves.

2. Add the juniper berries, mustard, honey and salt.

3. Cook uncovered over a medium heat, stir often with a wooden spoon and don't add more liquids: at first the vinegar and the onion and pear juices will be enough. When the cooking liquid has become syrupy and the mixture risks sticking, add a little water at a time and only when necessary; the chutney mustn't float.

4. Cook for about 30 minutes from boiling time: the pears should not become mushy. Add the mustard powder and the sliced dried figs halfway through cooking. When the chutney is ready, add the cognac and let evaporate for a minute before taking off the heat.

5. Pour the boiling chutney into a spotlessly clean glass jar, eliminate any air bubbles with a knife or a spoon and allow to cool before closing the jar. Keep it in the fridge, it will last a month.

Endive and mandarin chutney

TIME: 1 HOUR 15 MINUTES

150 ml/5 fl oz cider vinegar
80 g/just over 3 oz cane sugar
250 g/9 oz endive
2 knobs fresh ginger
250 g/9 oz mandarins
80 g/just over 3 oz shallots
2 cloves garlic
50 g/2 oz dried apricots
1 tablespoon golden syrup
grated zest of 1 unwaxed lemon
table salt
ground chilli pepper
1 small glass (50ml/1 ½ fl oz) rum
    or other dry liqueur

(the quantities of fruit and
vegetables are to be considered
without peelings)

1. Put the vinegar and sugar in a wide non-stick frying pan. Add the following, as they are ready:
- the peeled, washed and finely sliced endive and ginger
- the de-seeded and chopped mandarins (each segment chopped into 2-3 pieces)
- the peeled, washed and finely sliced shallots and garlic (remove the green part of the garlic if present)
- the sliced dried apricots.

2. Add the golden syrup, lemon zest and salt (do not exaggerate)

3. Cook uncovered over a medium heat, stir often with a wooden spoon and don't add more liquids: at first the vinegar and the fruit and vegetable juices will be enough. When the cooking liquid has become syrupy and the mixture risks sticking, add a little water at a time and only if necessary; the chutney mustn't float.

4. Cook for about 30–35 minutes from boiling time. Add the chilli pepper halfway through cooking. When the chutney is ready, add the rum and let evaporate for a minute before taking off the heat.

5. Pour the boiling chutney into a spotlessly clean glass jar, eliminate any air bubbles with a knife or a spoon and allow to cool before closing the jar. Keep it in the fridge, it will last a month.

chutney di
pere e fichi
alla senape

Chutney story

"There's a bra, out there!" exclaimed Ivor Critchley astonished, as he came in the back door. He would often return from his brisk morning walk through the woods - armed with his walking stick and military manner – with an account of his discoveries. They usually consisted of wild rabbits, deer, and species of birds he thought were extinct. Less often, near the path that went round the village, there was some human presence from outside the usual realm of village inhabitants: a new postman, a milkman's boy who had got stuck in the lorry, or a friend of Rev. Fitzwalter who was far from saintly.
But a bra, oh no, this was a sensational discovery.

Brenda and I looked at each other with raised eyebrows. She had been Ivor Critchley's wife for forty years, and knew her husband was a tad batty: he would drive his car as if it was an RAF plane, and collect dead flies under his paperweight, but – for all the kings of England! – all this didn't make him delusional. Moreover, there are delusions and delusions… That courteous retired gentleman had received the kind of education that prevented him from telling titillating tales, first thing in the morning: at least, not in front of a guest who hadn't yet turned eighteen, and had just arrived from Italy to perfect her English. We would never have usually abandoned our tea for a pheasant or a ditzy girl from Canterbury, but the extraordinary sighting of such an object made us get up from the table in unison.

Now, I know that "brassiere" is not exactly a word you'd expect to find in a cookery book, especially at Christmas. I also know that nowadays the term, even when in an appropriate context, risks sounding terribly obsolete, given that even the older generation call this kind of lady's item - independent of model or type – "lingerie". But, believe me, there is no other way of describing a gigantic pair of emerald green satin pointed cones, stitched to a band wide enough for a sumo wrestler. It was hanging among the branches of a bush with orange berries, just beyond the garden hedge.

Given the position, shape and perfect hold on the bush, to an ironical and somewhat eccentric eye (both characteristics that are generously present in human beings of the species "Britannica") they looked like a bird's nest, designed by an avant-garde architect with a propensity for psychedelic situations (they were all the rage, at that time). But not even under the effect of hallucinogenic mushrooms could they have been a titillating sight…

The image of three people surrounding a piece of underwear circumspectly, analysing it as Linneo would have done with a rare flower, was ridiculous. If a pheasant had passed at that moment, back from his morning walk through the woods (try to imagine a "species swap"…), he would have remarked to Lady Pheasant, waiting for him at home with a nice cup of tea, that he had witnessed an extremely strange scene indeed.

stories

The first humans to know about this event were Miss Perkins, a retired teacher, and her sister Dorothy (who, perhaps because she hadn't been a teacher but a children's nanny, was known simply as Dorothy, even though she was a Miss Perkins, too). As soon as they'd recovered from the initial shock, they agreed that the said item could not possibly belong to anyone in the village, and they could be "absolutely sure" of this as there were no more than two hundred inhabitants, and they knew each and every one of them. Moreover, how on earth had it got there? The only possible route, considering that it had blown in on the strange Kentish winds, was from the neighbouring cottage, but this was a far-fetched idea: because that beautiful run-down building, with its wooden beams and thatched roof, was William's house …

William was a poor devil, avoided by everyone because he did not wash as often as required, drank too much gin even if it wasn't a Friday, and welcomed social workers on their regular visits to him by booming "Stay away!" with the voice of an ogre. A self-styled artist, once he had thrown an easel at Reverend Fitzwalter, and his garden left much to be desired; but Brenda, who had preserved a certain affection for *maudit* artists, dating back to her roaring years spent in Paris as a model, maintained that he was a misunderstood artist. The austere Critch had a completely different idea, of course, but he managed to maintain a certain level of tolerance with him.

The only living beings of female gender to have frequented William were a cat and a parrot, so it was "scientifically proven" (the scientist was Gwenda Llewellyn, a prime authority on gossip) that the brassiere had nothing to do with him. In his sober past there had been a certain Margaret from a nearby village, but, according to Gordon the carpenter, that girl was the demonstration that God knew how to use a plain: had there been a re-kindling of the romance, any suspicion would never have fallen on her.

The fact remained that the discovery of the brassiere had unleashed unspeakable havoc in the village, and over the next few days, from the pub to the priory, the debate raged on as to its origins.
An official version was needed, because Edwina Calthorpe was to be married in a week's time, and it would not be the done thing for a member of the House of Lords to allow respectable guests at his daughter's wedding, with such a bizarre story hanging in the air (you know what it's like at weddings, one glass too many and everything comes out). The wise Reverend came up with an explanation, the most innocuous one for the handful of souls entrusted to his care: the brassiere must have belonged to the busty elephant tamer of the circus that had passed through the village a few days before. Edwina Calthorpe could tie the knot without any menacing shadows of brassieres on the horizon…

It was Brenda who finally solved the case, and it was all down to her sense of smell, that helped her to recognise the perfume of India. The daughter of a colonel of Her Majesty's army, she had played in the shade of mango trees as a child, run after monkeys as if they were cats, and taken trips in the jungle on the back of an elephant: certain details couldn't escape her…
"She's a girl: and she's Indian!" she exclaimed one afternoon, coming back in from the garden. "She's roasting spices to make chutney, and she's clearly an expert".

No-one ever found out exactly how the curvaceous Indian girl came to be in William's cottage: perhaps he had met her at a Social Services course they organised in Canterbury, to which he was regularly sent. Or she was a model for his eccentric pictures and he had "bought her from a catalogue", as Gwenda Llewellyn insinuated. Or maybe she was a gift from God, as Reverend Fitzwalter lovingly suggested.

stories

Or maybe it's simply that there's a chance for everybody, even those who have a dislike for shaving and keeping a nice garden, and if you can manage to grab it, the pieces of an unkempt existence can come back together as a life once more.

Timid lines of washing began to stretch between what had once been flowerbeds: gaudy garments billowed in the wind, like extra-large Tibetan prayer flags. They broke through the grey of autumn and announced to the world that William had stopped causing himself harm.

Nobody had yet seen her, it took several weeks until she managed to get over her shyness, but that she was Indian (and lived there…) could no longer be doubted: spicy aromas wafted out of their kitchen window, scents of India that only Brenda knew how to name and connect to a memory.

When I received her Christmas wishes there was also a photo in the envelope, taken from the bush with orange berries: William's house had a plastic Christmas tree in the garden, two little elephants blowing trumpets to the clouds, and a garland on the door.

stories

Slow-cooked

His Majesty *Bollito*

Bollito *has two fundamental ingredients: a trusty butcher and a few hours of your time.*
If you're not a veggie, a trusty butcher is one of the bedrocks of your kitchen… infinitely more important that any new-fangled gadget that doesn't ever let you get your hands dirty.
A good butcher will get hold of a real cotechino *(see p. 90), will not saddle you with the leanest meat for a pot roast, and when needed will fillet a chicken for you to perfection, making your favourite filling stay on its best behaviour. He'll make fresh hamburgers for you on request and will agree with you that cheek is often better than fillet, even if it costs half as much.*
He'll look at you kindly when you ask him to roll a duck breast, and when you order some tripe he'll give you his recipe.
If you haven't already got a butcher like this, go out and find one similar and order the meat for a perfect bollito:
a sumptuous mixed bollito *with all the meat cuts you need.*
It's important for you to know that it would be too much for just two people, so if this is your case, consider inviting someone else to join the company. Make sure they like eating slowly because bollito *requires time, beginning with its preparation; it is simple to make but needs to be cooked separately (in at least four different large pans).*
If the butcher has all the above qualities, is seventy-eight years old and his name is Vittorio, he will tell you the cooking times for each piece of meat… and he'll want to know how it went, too.

Note: *bollito* is a typical dish of the Northern part of Italy based on different meat cuts boiled (= *bollito*) with vegetables in abundant water.

Shopping list for 6-8 people

1 600 g/1.3 lb *cotechino* (very large pork sausage)	1/2 chicken (a hen is better)
1 kg tongue	1 kg/2.2 lb onions
1 *testina* weighing 600 g/1.3 lb	1.2 kg/2.2 lb carrots
1 small piece of flank steak	1 large whole celery
1 knee bone	1 bay leaf
1 piece of muscle of about 1.2-1.4 kg/ just over 2½ lb-3 lb	2 sundried tomatoes
	cooking salt

Testina

A testina *weighing half a kilo (or just over a pound), has usually the same weigh as a bigger meat cut, which means the netting that encloses it opens on at least one side. If you want it to keep its shape to cut it easily and present it elegantly, you have to make sure it doesn't slip out while cooking. Tie it with kitchen string (I have even used strong embroidery thread if necessary) without pulling too tightly; pass the string more times over the open side of the netting, making a half knot between one circle and another (as you would for sausages). In this way, the* testina *will resemble one of those string-tied roasts...*

TIME: ABOUT 2½ HOURS

1 piece of *testina* weighing about
   600 g/1.2 lb
3 carrots
2 celery sticks
2 medium onions
Salt

1. Peel and rinse the vegetables; put them in a large high-sided pan.

2. Add the *testina*, cover with plenty of cold water and a little salt. Cook over a medium heat for about 2 hours from boiling point. Keep it well covered with water. It's ready when you feel it's tender when pricked with a sharp knife.

3. Remove the netting from the *testina* and cut into slices of about 1 cm/0.3". Just one in each plate, because its gelatinous consistency is more appreciated in small doses, and really hot…

Note: *testina* is the head of the veal rolled inside a string netting.

Tongue

TIME: ABOUT 2½ HOURS

1 tongue weighing about 1kg/1.2 lb
3 carrots
2 celery stalks
2 medium onions
Salt

1. Peel and rinse the vegetables; put them in a large high-sided pan.

2. Rinse the tongue under cold running water and put it in the pan with the vegetables, plenty of water and a little salt. Cook over a medium heat for about 2 hours from boiling point. The water should cover it well; add more if necessary.

3. It's ready when you feel it's tender when pricked with a sharp knife.

4. Leave to cool a little, then eliminate the tough skin and cut into slices. If you are not sure you'll eat it all, remove the skin from the part you intend to slice and leave the rest under its skin (in a container sealed with cling film) in the fridge. According to Signor Vittorio, it will keep for about ten days.

Cotechino

*"Look at that beauty; stunning! It looks just like Sophia Loren's!", exclaimed the satisfied butcher.
"I don't quite understand…". "Take a look at that cotechino's belly button!", and he pointed to the knot tied with
string like a seal. It was just perfect. He was immensely satisfied indeed with a beatific smile stamped across his old
face. I couldn't tell you if it was all down to Sophia Loren's belly button or the* cotechino *itself (it was probably
the evocative nature of both working in perfect harmony), but if I had learned one thing that day, it was that the
knot is important. I'm not suggesting you get all emotional over a great big nude pork sausage, but check the knot
before bringing it home as it can tell you a lot… Leave pre-cooked* cotechino *to the feeble: no packaged shortcuts for
us, especially at Christmas! So make time to find a* cotechino *that is just right. The skin should be made of pig gut
rather than synthetic material (a butcher who is attentive to such details will put the best meat inside, too) and ask
your butcher for the correct cooking time: it will be much longer than a pre-packed* cotechino *for the feeble.
After all, Christmas is a time of expectation…*

TIME: ABOUT 2 HOURS

1 *cotechino* **weighing about
600 g/1.2 lb**
2 carrots
1 celery stick
1 medium onion
1 bay leaf

1. Peel and rinse the vegetables and the bay leaf; put them all in a high-sided pan.

2. Prick the *cotechino* with a pin in 2-3 points. It's not a voodoo ritual but prevents it from splitting while cooking. The fact that it's not voodoo doesn't mean you can massacre your *cotechino* by stabbing it all over with a fork; it would suffer and so would you, watching all its aromatic contents spurt out of a horrendous gash. So just a very few pinpricks will be enough. Put the *cotechino* in the pan and cover it with cold water.

3. Cook it uncovered over minimum heat for about 2 hours. Despite its rough appearance, the *cotechino* has a delicate skin that needs sweet and calm cooking water, so no salt and no waves.
Take it out of the cooking water as soon as it is ready. The water will be full of the fat that the *cotechino* has lost. Keep the water for reheating later. If you're not eating it immediately, put the *cotechino* in a high-sided container (a casserole dish is perfect) and seal with cling film, making sure the latter doesn't touch the *cotechino*.

Note: *cotechino* is a typical Italian large seasoned pork sausage. It's usually eaten at Christmastime and served with lentils and purée.

"The hen has to be ready for the stock like a bride for her husband... beautiful!", said Delfina as she sat on the stuffed cellar chair plucking the next winged creature in line. A feathered friend should never reach the pan without having had a good session with a beauty therapist; whether it's a hen, duck, chicken or capon, excess fat and superfluous feathers just won't do. Eliminate any flaps of skin and fat that are not directly attached to meat and check that there are no small feathers, especially on the wings or near the legs. If there is the slightest sign of any hairiness, light the hob and use the flame to burn it off. Cover the area with foil, throw open the window and when you have finished, try out the power of pot-pourri on p.181.

Stock and its meats

In my childhood memories, stock made using a capon was always number one. It was adored by my father. He insisted that to make the best tortellini *possible, only a stock that had sacrificed the virility of a cockerel would do. Number two was hen stock, but the hens we used had to have a certain pedigree; this meant they had to come from Delfina's farmyard. The mixed meat stock came from a slightly less aristocratic category, firstly because we bought the meat at the butcher's; secondly because it became a stock only after having carried out its primary function of cooking the meats entrusted to its care. Over the years the population of Delfina's farmyard became somewhat depleted, no-one wanted her hens or capons anymore except us, so the mixed meat stock went up a notch in the top ten. Capon held first position (also considering that finding a sample of this cathegory became more and more difficult), but we began to like the butcher's meats almost more than that of Delfina's hens. Of course, the stock was just a pretext; the real dish was the* bollito…

TIME: ABOUT 2½ HOURS

1 piece of muscle weighing about 1.2-
    1.4 kg/just over 2 ½ lb-3lb
1 small piece of flank steak
1 knee bone
½ chicken (or better, hen)
2 sundried tomatoes
3 carrots
3 celery sticks
1 medium onion

1. Peel and rinse the vegetables and put them in a large pan with very high sides. Rinse the bone and put it in the pan with the flank steak and plenty of cold water.

2. Switch on the largest hob ring, bring the contents to the boil and add the muscle and the chicken. Remove the foam, especially at the beginning. Then lower the heat, cover the pan leaving a small crack for the steam to escape and forget all about your stock for about an hour/an hour and a half.
You just need to check from time to time that it doesn't overflow and that all the meat is covered with water (if you need to top it up, go ahead, but don't overdo it; just move the meat so that none of it sticks out of the water).

3. Next, start checking if the various meats are cooked, with the tip of a sharp knife (its effects are less devastating than a fork…). If one of them is cooked before the others, don't leave it there to disintegrate; take it out and leave it in a covered container with a little stock.

4. When the stock starts to boil calculate roughly a couple of hours of cooking time. If you're going to eat the *bollito* straightaway, keep the meat hot in its stock until you are ready to serve.

5. Stock is a precious resource. If you have some to spare, it can be used as a base for a lot of different dishes, especially at Christmas. You can use it to cook *tortellini*, make a *risotto* (if you use proper stock, it's infinitely better) and prepare meatballs (this is one of my friend the butcher's tips; a few spoonfuls of stock in the mixture make it softer). Strain the stock through a colander and keep it in the fridge (with a lid on if you don't wish it to absorb strong aromas). The next day, eliminate the layer of solid fat that will have formed on the surface; you'll discover – if your butcher has given you the right meats – that the stock will have transformed itself into a wonderful jelly.

recipes

Jellied ham terrine

Don't tell the butcher that you've ordered two pork shanks for boiling. Only tell him if he is a true butcher and when there is no trace of anyone posh in the shop at the time. I'm telling you this because in Italy pork shanks are exclusively for roasting. That's all. It's such a shame. Now back to our jambon; in Gallic kitchens – such as Thierry's, where this recipe comes from – it would be part of an Easter picnic. I always joke with him that it takes a touch of grandeur to call prosciutto (ham) "shank", and he replies that there's only one "ham" and it should be called "ham" in every language; all the rest are cuts of meat, not unique recipes! With his approach things can change, such as adding a terrine of jambon-that-isn't-a-ham-despite-its-name to buffets for friends, even at Christmas. No-one has ever complained.

TIME: 3½-4 HOURS + RESTING IN THE FRIDGE

MAKES A TERRINE OF 15 X 8 X 7 CM/ 6 X 3 X 2.7"

2 rindless pork shanks
1 beef brisket
½ bottle white wine
3 tablespoons cider (or white) vinegar
1 large, or 2 small, onions
2 celery stalks
3 carrots
2 bay leaves
1 sprig thyme
2 sprigs parsley
10 peppercorns

FOR THE TERRINE
Gelatine cubes or powder
A large handful of parsley

❄ *A jelly is not a jelly unless it is transparent. A murky jelly is most unpleasant to the eye, and because the eye tastes the dish before the tongue, it won't even be worth putting on the table. The cooking juices of the flanks should be filtered carefully; get a sieve, spoon and a fine tablecloth and be patient as this step is slow and quite laborious.*

1. Put the flanks and the bone in a large pan (where they can float happily). Add the wine, vinegar, pepper and plenty of water to cover the meat by a few cm/an inch or so. Peel and rinse the vegetables, cut the onion into wedges, cut the celery and carrots into large pieces. Rinse the aromatic herbs. Throw everything into the pan with the meat.

2. Leave to boil over a medium heat for 2/2 ½ hours until the meat comes away from the bone easily (but try not to let it disintegrate). Remove and drain the shanks, put them aside. Drain the stock through a colander and when it is cool, put it in the fridge (cover it so that it doesn't absorb other aromas).

3. Now it's time to concentrate on the flanks. Remove the meat with your hands and take off the skin, as well as any remaining nerves and fat. Be as accurate as you can; try to maintain the pieces of meat as intact as possible. When you have finished, put the meat in the fridge covered with cling film.

4. After a few hours (even a day after), remove the fat from the stock, eliminating the layer that will have formed on the surface. Underneath, you'll find a soft jelly; put it over the heat, allow to melt and then filter the liquid (you'll need to arm yourself with patience; this may take a while). Put it back over the heat and reduce it by letting it simmer for 10 minutes. Measure it out in a graduated jug and add an amount of gelatine preparation equal to half the quantity indicated on the instructions (if you need a cube for every half litre of liquid, add half a cube; the bone in the stock will have done the remaining work).

5. Line a tin with a double layer of cling film. Be precise, because it would be shame if your terrine came out perfectly transparent but lumpy!

6. Break the meat up with your hands, following the direction of the fibres (the pieces don't need to be regular). Wash the parsley and chop it finely; sprinkle a thin layer over the bottom of the tin and add the rest to the meat, mixing well.

7. Pour over a stream of gelatine (just warm) on the bottom of the tin, fill it to half way with pieces of meat and pour over more gelatine. Repeat the operation until the tin is full, pressing the meat down delicately; make sure the gelatine is evenly distributed.

8. Put it in the fridge and wait a few hours for the gelatine to set before turning it out onto the serving dish. Serve with a colourful salad and slices of toasted bread.

Guancino in vin brûlé
(Beef cheek in mulled wine)

Glory be to guancino*, to butchers able to procure it as it should be (that is, not frozen), and to their customers who are brave enough to order a* guancino*. Love for such a dish could induce you to buy yourself – or ask for – a really super cast iron pan for Christmas; it will last a lifetime and you can make so many things in it (including bread). The list of ingredients for this recipe is very long simply because at Christmas I like to marinate* guancino *in a true* vin brûlé *and believe me, it's worth it. What's more, cooking with wine is not a time for bringing out* bouchonné *or acidic wines, nor is it advisable to try out any of that dubious-looking dishwater in tetra pak cartons. Get yourself a good bottle at a reasonable price (there are lots of wines that are worth discovering, and in such occasions too) and enjoy the pleasure of popping the cork.*

TIME: 2-2½ HOURS + A NIGHT
MARINATING IN THE FRIDGE

MAKES ENOUGH FOR 2 PEOPLE IF
IT'S THE ONLY MAIN COURSE, FOR
4 PEOPLE IF THERE ARE OTHER
DISHES

1 beef cheek (about 700 g/1½ lb)
½ bottle Barolo (or other still red
   wine)
10 cloves
10 peppercorns
1 star anise
2 cinnamon sticks of about 6 cm/
   2.3"
Nutmeg
The zest of 1 unwaxed mandarin
¼ unwaxed apple
1 large carrot
1 celery stick
2 shallots
3 bay leaves
1 sprig rosemary
3-4 juniper berries
3 tablespoons extra-virgin olive oil
1 tablespoon butter
Vegetable stock granules
Salt
Freshly milled black pepper

1. First prepare the *vin brûlé* for the marinade. Put the wine with the cloves, pepper, star anise, cinnamon, a generous grating of nutmeg, the mandarin zest and apple wedges cut into 3 pieces (skin on) into a pan. Simmer over a very low heat for about a quarter of an hour. Strain through a sieve, pressing the apple and mandarin zest so as not to lose any juice.

2. Peel and rinse the carrot, celery and shallots. Rinse the bay leaves and rosemary. Add the carrots and celery that you have chopped widthways, the sliced shallots, the bay leaves, rosemary and the crushed juniper berries (one bash of a meat hammer for each one) to the filtered *vin brûlé*.

3. Transfer the marinade into an iron, glass or ceramic container that will fit the beef cheek as well. The meat must be covered by the liquid as much as possible. If this is difficult, turn the meat from time to time. Seal with cling film and put it in the fridge overnight.

4. The next day, put the oil and butter into a pan, add the drained beef cheek and brown it on all sides. You only need 5 minutes; turn it several times and keep it balanced with a couple of spoons (don't poke it with a fork) to make sure it browns all over. Add salt and pepper before you give it a final turn.

5. Now add the marinade (remove only the rosemary if you don't like the idea of all those needles) and leave to cook over a very low heat with the lid on, for about an hour and a half (a good butcher will know the right cooking times; trust his directions). Add a few vegetable stock granules halfway through cooking time and a little water if needed; the sauce should be dense, reduced and really aromatic.

6. Serve the beef cheek piping hot, accompanied by mashed pumpkin or potato. It is transformed into a truly unique dish – sumptuous, especially for celebration days – if you serve it with a good risotto (made with proper stock) or polenta.

recipes

Duck breast with chestnuts in Armagnac

Duck and goose have gone much the same way as the Pyrenean ibex; almost extinct on Italian tables. This feathered disappearance is one that I cannot resign myself to; when I was a child, every farmyard teemed with ducks, geese, turkeys and guinea fowl as well as chickens (transformed into majestic capons when needed) and cockerels. Today there are only chickens and turkeys that become plastic-packaged breasts and thighs; they all taste pretty much the same. Having savoured duck ragù for gnocchi, roast goose and duck eggs (Delfina used them to make tagliatelle), I have a real passion for these types of meat. I generally make good use of them over New Year, inviting friends over to keep us company. Seeing as we live quite a distance from our butcher, I arrange for him to send me a couple of cases of meat, agreeing on every minimal detail beforehand by phone. "Can you find some blueberries for the venison?", "How about some chestnuts for the duck? Don't worry, I'll send you some stock to bind the meatballs...", he says, thoughtfully. Whenever I open his packages I always find some chopped herbs from his vegetable garden, a Mantua pumpkin (if I ask for one of these from a local greengrocer I might as well have requested something carnivorous), and naturally a cotechino, pork loin and at least one duck or goose. Then I spend two days in my kitchen transforming all of it into a wonderful New Year's Eve dinner, and I feel happy...

TIME: 2½ HOURS + A NIGHT
MARINATING IN THE FRIDGE

FOR 4-6 PEOPLE

1 duck breast of about 800 g/1.7 lb
A few slices of bacon
Vegetable granules

FOR THE FILLING
80-100 g/3-4 oz pre-sliced dark bread
30 g/just over 1 oz butter
1 small onion
1 large shallot
2 teaspoons cane sugar
150 g/6 oz pre-cooked chestnuts
20 g/just under 1 oz walnut kernels
3-4 dried figs
4-5 sprigs fresh thyme
1 egg
1 small (50 ml/1 ½ fl oz) glass
Armagnac

FOR THE MARINADE
4 carrots
2 celery stalks
5-6 shallots
2 bay leaves
A few sprigs of fresh thyme
About 100 ml/3.4 fl oz Armagnac
Salt
Freshly milled black pepper

1. Cut the bread into 1 cm/0.3" cubes and fry them in a pan for 4-5 minutes with half of the butter; they should be crunchy outside and soft inside. Add salt and pepper and put to one side.

2. Chop the shallot and onion very finely and cook them slowly in the pan with the rest of the butter (first eliminate any bread residues). When they are transparent, add the sugar and, when melted and turned amber, take away from the heat.

3. Crush the chestnuts with a fork (don't mush them into a purée, though, as those little pieces are delicious...). Break up the walnuts and cut the figs into 5 mm/0.1" squares (if they are very dry, leave them to soak for 15 minutes in warm water).

4. Put the chestnuts, walnuts, figs, thyme, onion, shallot and crumbled croutons into a bowl. Mix and adjust the salt and pepper (be brave...). Add the egg, a sprinkling of Armagnac and the filling is ready.

5. Place the filling in the centre of the duck breast, as if it is a *cotechino* (you don't have to spread it out), and roll it up tight leaving the skin on the outside. Place the bacon on the skinless part (see note) and tie the roll with kitchen string.

6. Peel and rinse the vegetables and aromatic herbs for the marinade; cut the carrots and celery widthways and the shallot in half. Put everything in a container that will also fit the duck breast as immersed as possible. Add the Armagnac then the rolled up seasoned breast. Leave to marinate overnight in the fridge, turning and rolling it in the liquid from time to time.

7. Remove the meat from its marinade, transfer to a pyrex dish and bake it without adding anything else in a preheated oven at 150°C/300°F for about 20 minutes; turn it after the first ten minutes. Take out of the oven, moisten with marinade (including the vegetables) and continue to cook for about an hour/an hour and 15 minutes, raising the oven temperature to 180°C/350°F. Turn it a couple of times and baste with hot stock made with the vegetable granules.

8. Once cooked, cut into slices and serve with a mash.

Ask your butcher to cut open the duck breast like a book, and to remove half of the skin, leaving the other half attached (the rolled up breast should be half covered with skin, half with bacon).

recipes

The winter
vegetable garden

The Christmas play

The Christmas play was the event of the year at the Montessori nursery. It meant weeks of preparation for the nuns, mums and children, but it would never have entered anyone's head to pull out of such a commitment. The organisation was complex, but perfect: there was rigorous allocation of tasks, and we all shared the same goals with a fierce sense of joint responsibility.

All the nuns were missionaries, so they were capable of doing jobs that no mother could have managed. In those days, what is now known as DIY - and ladies are just as competent as their husbands - was labelled "men's work" (meaning males who were specialised in the field or had some marked innate ability, which, at the nursery, referred to a small subgroup of fathers). So, for us children to watch girls in long skirts casually tinkering about with a saw and a hammer, and who never hit their fingers when banging in nails, was an amazing sight, akin to seeing acrobats performing at a circus: something that made us believe they were special, and not only as handmaidens of God.

The nuns were our superheroes, and we often wondered where their mysterious strength came from. My brother said it came from Africa, from having seen all those big, dangerous animals. But I knew that mums could go to Africa, too, but this didn't mean they would come back knowing how to bang in a nail with a hammer. One of our friends had gone to Africa with her husband, and they had also gone on safari (even though it was obvious she already knew a lot about ferocious animals, as she often wore leopardskin), but for a birthday party she had stuck some paper garlands up with drawing pins, and they had fallen onto the cake. This had all convinced me that the origin of the nuns' superpowers lay in the one thing that distinguished them from our mothers: the veil. And I would have given anything to experience the thrill of trying one on for an "official" occasion…

There were very few "official" occasions in the life of a little girl, let's say just one: the Christmas play. The script, which the nuns adapted every year, offered a wide range of veil opportunities. For a start, all the shepherds had a veil but they had to be boys, hold a stick to guide the sheep and, what's more, the brownish tablecloth they wore on their head was far from elegant. Then there were milkmaids and farmers, with baskets full of vegetables carried like handbags, wearing veils of various shades… not exactly very beautiful.

And finally there was The Veil, the one of the highest level (given the close kinship relation with God) that shone with its own light at centre stage: the one that the Madonna wore. Jesus' mum was a familiar presence to us: we prayed to her before break time, and we would go and find her in Mother Superior's airless chapel, where there was a terrible smell of used candles and, even worse, we had to be quiet, but thank goodness we only went there for important occasions.

stories

Then there was the printed Madonna, the one on the prayer cards that the vicar gave us along with others of children holding lilies, knights spearing dragons and girls with their hands together talking to angels: all with a halo above their head, of course. I loved this Madonna, but she always came to a tragic end: I would forget about her in the pockets of my pinafore, and Delfina would find her all crumpled up with bits of crayon and biscuits, when she put it in the washing machine.

But my favourite Madonna was the one about the same height as my sister, who stood (the Madonna, not my sister…) beneath a glass bell in the room where we played. She was smiling and more fashionable than the others because she had plastic flowers necklaces, and she didn't need candles: we placed small jars of diluted watercolours in front of her, and she was much happier - we knew from her expression… - among all those colours. She had the most beautiful veil, or maybe it seemed that way to me because you could see it from the back, too, which you couldn't on the one in Mother Superior's chapel (she had imprisoned her Madonna with her shoulders against the wall). You couldn't see the back of the veil on the vicar's prayer cards either, as when you turned them over there was a prayer on the back.

That white veil, which, even though it was made of painted plaster you could see it was elegant from the way it fell, was used as the model for the leading actress' costume in the Christmas play. It was a coveted role but, as you may understand, could not be given to just anybody. It wasn't just a case of rocking the baby in a plywood manger: you had to remember your lines, move like a consummate actress, speak clearly. You needed a high level of psychological endurance – or rather, a bit of nerve – as well, to remain unmoved during applause or the emotional outbursts of grandparents.

Not to brag, but I had all these necessary qualities. Our mother always made us sing in the car to keep us occupied, and our vast repertoire - from alpine songs to Gianni Morandi, and even a few French rhymes - was in all respects a mnemonic exercise.
As far as gestures were concerned, I would watch *Canzonissima* on Saturday evenings, and act it out with my brother on the landing every afternoon. Our shows were very professional: we danced, presented, and even ended with the theme song in front of a cheering audience consisting of our mother and Delfina, sitting on two chairs they'd brought from the kitchen.
Clear diction wasn't a problem either, as in our house it was forbidden to allow even the slightest hint of dialect to pass our lips: if Mamma heard us distort any words – it happened when we played "Delfina and Gambucci", instead of "cowboys and Indians" - she would make us repeat the sentence "in perfect Italian".

If I should be grateful for all these qualities, it should be to my tirelessly attentive mother (who will no doubt be filled with pride on reading this, and maybe even shed a tear, we all know what mums are like). But there's another quality I have the good Lord to thank for: my nerve, which I had been given in generous quantities, was a gift of nature.

There's another event to add to this CV of mine: six months earlier I had played the part of Italy, nonetheless, in a patriotic play which had come from Suor Rosetta's prolific pen. A crown made of golden card on my head and a standard in my hand, I had stood completely still for a good three quarters of an hour, wrapped in a gigantic Italian flag.

The difficulty of this role was not so much putting up with the boredom, but more desperately trying

not to burst out laughing every time I looked at the fearless soldiers next to me: my cousin and another boy, wearing ladies' swimming caps stuck to their forehead and strapped tightly under their chin, were a hilarious sight.

The Christmas play had an altogether different poignancy, beginning with its soundtrack. We only had to sing "*Tu scendi dalle stelle*" for us to feel as if we were really in that stable in the freezing cold, and not just because two nuns had gone up a ladder to drop confetti from a height as if it was snow.

There was a sense of expectation in those Christmas carols, a certainty that the holiday would be wonderful, full of cousins, grandparents, games and surprises under the tree. There would be everything we could wish for and more: the competition to see who could be the best behaved, the risk of getting coal in one's stocking, the mystery of the *Befana* and Father Christmas, and… yes, heaps of good things to eat, too. However, I'm digressing, so let's get back to the electric atmosphere of the Christmas play preparations.

In the weeks before the event, the nursery looked like the Yangzee dam construction site: huge tasks were carried out inside its walls. The convent carpenter was given the responsibility of structural jobs, such as the barn, a shooting star with just the right inclination without risk of falling, trees as tall as people, outlines of camels; all the other jobs were done by the children and the nuns, jointly (but not necessarily in that order).

Sheets of polystyrene, cardboard, coloured card, ribbons, craft paper, pieces of material, drawing pins, scissors, staple guns, felt tip pens, crayons, watercolours… I think you've got the drift of it: we're talking about seriously strong emotions here. Rivers of PVA glue flowed in full stream, like beer at the Oktoberfest. As for glitter, an absolute must for a truly authentic Christmas, we had traces of it stuck to us until at least Shrove Tuesday.

Costume makers and drama assistants worked from home. Mamma made us learn our parts by heart, while Nonna, who knew how to sew, transformed lengths of material into fantastic costumes. For special accessories such as self-propelled wings, halos and crowns of stars, we could ask Gambucci, but only if we needed some iron wire or a few screws.

That year my costume did not leave much room for creativity: the rules were quite prescriptive when it came to holy characters, and the nuns – to avoid any surprises at the last minute – provided precise iconographic references. In my case, Nonna had to create a "Madonna of the Glass Bell" costume, the one with the small jars of watercolours instead of candles: number one in my list of favourite Madonnas. The veil consisted of swathes of white satin, and they'd bought double the quantity, that year, because another costume was needed for the second actor in the house: my brother.

He had been sent to the nursery younger than most – the nuns had welcomed him, in spite of the rules - because our sister had come into the world only 22 months after him, and Delfina had her hands full at home while our mother was at school. He was the smallest of the whole Montessori nursery, he had two kissable chubby pink cheeks, and huge eyes that made him look like such a good boy whatever he'd been up to: he was a natural candidate for the role of an angel.

Since he was so young, he wasn't given any lines: as a cherub, he only had to stand still, just behind the

Madonna but in a slightly raised position, and look towards Baby Jesus. As angels don't by nature have their feet on the ground, and homemade wings can play tricks (look what happened to poor Icarus), the nuns had specifically designed a small toddler-proof pedestal for him, on which he had practised standing still.

The day of the play arrived. The rhythm increased, adrenalin rushes ran through children's bodies with shivers (and you can never understand whether they're shivers of pleasure or terror). The nuns, who were experts in children's mechanisms, had sent us all to the bathroom, before we started (there was always at least one poor victim of his own emotions).
The scenery – palm trees, sand dunes, and a far-off oasis under a watercolour blue sky filled with glittery stars – was grand, stuff that would make the local amateur dramatics society jealous. The audience was distributed according to age: grandparents and the convent carpenter (who were coeval) in the front row, pregnant mums on the wooden benches, and everyone else in the gallery.

My brother was behind me. He was an angel perfectly in keeping with the costume's requirements: a white tunic with tiny stars, a halo of silver wire (Gambucci's masterpiece), and cardboard wings secretly anchored to his trouser braces. As for me, my veil was magnificent, and luckily it sometimes slipped down, so that I could throw it back over my shoulder with a quick movement of my hand. I'd never seen a Madonna do this before (it was not my fault if the available ones were all completely still), only my mother, who never wore a veil but did wear certain beautiful shawls on summer evenings. It wasn't exactly the gesture of a nun either, but after all mine was no ordinary veil: it was extra-special…

The curtain went up and the show began. It was a tried and tested screenplay, as Christmas is always the story of a child who is born in a stable in the company of an ox and a donkey, and his parents, of course. And however much the nuns could change the number of shepherds or angels according to how many children were enrolled in the nursery, the number of Kings had to be three, the shooting star one, and you couldn't exactly have a surprise ending. With such a well known script, the audience's attention was fixed on the actors.

"The nun said you must look at Baby Jesus in the manger. Promise me you'll concentrate and don't fall over, ok?" I had told my brother. With his plump red cheeks like rosy apples, he had lowered his big eyes in obedience.

Christmas plays, as you know, are always long: they must give everyone an opportunity and that's what makes them so wonderful. I played my part smoothly and even Giuseppe, who had a bit of a lisp, performed beautifully. The Three Kings arrived with shoulder bag-style camels, there was a slight problem with their bows but the gold, frankincense and myrrh (three biscuit tins covered with foil) were warmly welcomed, anyway. Shepherds, fishermen and farmers left all of their gifts at our feet: a heap of vegetables from the kitchen, about ten plastic fish, and three two-dimensional cardboard sheep, that looked like bathmats but made us so proud because we had made them ourselves.

It was towards the end that I realized something was not going quite according to the script. It started with a hum of whispers in the audience, then grandparents and mothers were overheard talking about a special angel. There came a clicking of cameras in my direction… I continued to position my veil but… me?!?… I was no angel…

Snowflakes fell in handfuls from the top of the ladder, while Suor Rosetta threw herself into "*Tu scendi dalle stelle*" on the pianola. I grabbed my chance and turned round to see what all the fuss was about.

A child-angel not yet three years old, standing on the top of a wooden pedestal that had been dressed up as a cloud, had fallen asleep. The concentration necessary for him to keep his eyes on the manger had transformed itself gradually into drowsiness, until even his eyebrows had drooped… followed by his head, that lolled forward due to the weight of his cheeks. His halo had ended up sliding onto his face, held on only by an ear that had turned bright red like the butcher's-broom berries that adorned the room, because of the heat. With one wing higher than the other – even braces slip, if you don't stand up straight – it was a miracle he hadn't fallen on the floor. He slept soundly, on his feet like a horse, and he was the most angelic angel you could possibly imagine.

There was nothing I could do but hope that he didn't land on me, if the flash of a camera suddenly woke him up.

I saw my mother being complimented by other members of the audience, because such a performance had never been seen before. "Look how clever that little boy is! He looks just like a real sleeping angel…"

It was inevitable: the play ended with jubilant applause, just for him. "What a lovely boy… - exclaimed the grandparents - he's the youngest of all of them and he was so good, right till the end! Well done, Signora, you have a true actor in your house!"

There was no final theme song, the nuns weren't familiar with *Canzonissima*. We did, however, sing the last carol altogether until the pianola chords gradually faded out, then a roar of hands clapped endlessly and there was a chorus of clicks… So, not exactly the usual calm awakening my brother was used to at home. He burst into tears, and they were not tears of emotion for all the compliments he received: he was only a little boy who wanted to sleep and had been woken up. And what's more, he didn't care one jot about being an angel, the most wonderful angel ever to have set foot on that stage.

There isn't a single photo of that afternoon in which he isn't crying desperately, his red cheeks streaked with great big tears, a lop-sided halo, droopy wings and braces. As for me, well, you can imagine: after all those dreams, all that hard work acting and the expectations of my veil, I had been completely upstaged by someone who had fallen asleep quite by chance… There isn't a single photo of that afternoon in which I'm not showing an expression of sheer irritation.

I believe, though, that there sure were some superpowers in my veil. My brother had managed to stay on his pedestal without falling off during his long deep sleep, and this was a miraculous occurrence. As for me, no-one has ever been able to explain why I'm the only person in our family who thoroughly enjoys sawing and hammering. Without once hitting a finger: just like the nuns…

Pumpkin purée and...

Whatever you wish to make with it, pumpkin acquires an amazing flavour after roasting.
Don't be afraid to sprinkle it with just a touch of cane sugar, even if you're making a savoury dish; it works like blusher on the cheeks of a pretty girl, highlighting beauty without being too heavy. Talking of comparisons, I should point out that pumpkins, like girls, are not all the same. If we take those from in and around Mantua, they are in a class of their own. Prepare yourself for a long courtship if you want to win their heart: they are quite tough-skinned.
If you don't give up at your first attempt (which I wholeheartedly suggest), you'll discover a fine, creamy consistency that is sweet but never sickly… the quintessence of femininity in vegetable form. Neapolitan pumpkins are of notable value but are not quite classy enough to create the base of a main course.
Their skin comes away easily but some filaments run through the pulp, the consistency is rather lumpy and the initial sweetness leaves a slightly acidic aftertaste, so make sure you bring home exactly the right pumpkin for your recipe.
As far as girls are concerned, relax: Eternal Father has distributed the tough ones (and here I refer not only to their skin) more fairly than pumpkins. They can be found in Naples and Mantua, and all around the world.

TIME: 1 HOUR 15 MINUTES

SERVES 4-5 PEOPLE

500 g/1 lb cleaned pumpkin
2 tablespoons extra-virgin olive oil
1 level teaspoon table salt
1 teaspoon cane sugar
150 g/6 oz fresh whipping cream

1. Preheat the oven to 200°C/400°F and line with parchment paper a baking tray or casserole dish wide enough to accommodate the pumpkin in one single layer.

2. Wash, dry and cut the pumpkin into slices 4-5 mm/0.1-2" thick. Lay the slices in the casserole dish, sprinkle with olive oil, add salt and sugar. Quickly mix, then bake for about 40 minutes. The pumpkin should be tender and soft when you touch it with a fork (an infallible test), but don't burn it: a mash filled with black spots is not a pleasant sight.

3. Place the pumpkin in the container of a hand blender and reduce to a fine purée with the help of the cream. You may not be able to do this in one whizz, so work the mixture several times, using more cream as necessary (pumpkin on its own is very compact).

4. When the single quantities are ready, put them into a pan, which you will use to reheat the purée when you are ready to serve. Adjust the seasoning as needed.

❄ *From 500 g/1 lb raw pumpkin you should get about 450 g/just under a lb of cooked pumpkin, which requires more or less 1/3 of its weight in cream. However, the eye often works better than the weighing scales in these cases, so have a good look at it!*

❄ *I usually accompany a pumpkin purée with a classic potato mash and a purée of broccoli and gorgonzola: they make a delicious trio.*

... pumpkin soufflé

A soufflé works much in the same way as a hot air balloon or a Chinese lantern; hot air inflates a canopy of cream which rises, with a little uncertainty at first but then more confidently.
The oven must be really hot for the magic to work, and the egg whites must be whipped to perfection. Then...
sit back and enjoy the performance! It won't last long, in fact it's almost momentary. If you are preparing single portions, it's a good idea to gather some friends in your kitchen so that they can admire the moment of crowning splendour before helping you serve... and if the soufflé has already sagged when you put it on the table, your friends can still sink their spoons in with great satisfaction.

TIME: 1 HOUR 15 MINUTES + 1 HOUR
IF YOU HAVE TO PREPARE THE
PUMPKIN

SERVES 6 PEOPLE AS A MAIN COURSE,
OR 12 AS A SMALL ENTRÉE

50 g/2 oz butter (plus a knob of
butter for the moulds)
3 shallots
50 g/2 oz all-purpose flour (plus a
little for the moulds)
350 ml/just under 12 fl oz whole
milk
200 g/8 oz baked pumpkin reduced
to a purée (see pumpkin purée
recipe on p. 109)
Nutmeg
60 g/just over 2 oz grated pecorino
cheese
Table salt
3 whole eggs plus 2 egg whites

❄ *Talking of containers, it's useful to know that a soufflé can rise just as happily from a coffee cup or a deep narrow bowl, but it's important to check in advance that the receptacle can withstand the heat of the oven. Now, here's a little secret: when I need to make a large number of them, I use glass candlesticks. Designed to withstand a flame, they've become best friends with my mini-soufflés!*

1. Preheat the oven to 220°C/430°F. Generously grease the moulds, throw in a little flour and turn in your hands to make it stick, then knock away any excess. Don't leave any fingermarks near the edge, because they would anchor the soufflé as it rises, and that is exactly what you don't need.

2. Peel the shallots and chop them finely, then cook them in a pan with the butter. When they are transparent, add the flour, mixing to prevent the roux from sticking (if you're asking yourself what a "roux" is, it's that sticky ball that has just formed before your very eyes; don't get distracted now, or it'll stick in a nanosecond).

3. Remove from the heat and add the milk a little at a time, mixing thoroughly. If you're not used to making béchamel sauces, it may seem impossible that this great blob can be transformed into a fine sauce, but have faith! It will happen, as long as you keep mixing after every addition of milk. When the only protuberances on the surface of your béchamel are the pieces of shallot, put it back on the heat and allow it to thicken, mixing continuously.

4. Add the pumpkin, pecorino, nutmeg and salt. Separate the egg yolks from the whites, add the yolks to the béchamel and mix again.

5. Now concentrate on the most important step in the creation of a soufflé: whipping the egg whites. I suggest to whisk them by hand, because it's the best way to avoid overworking them. Five whites are quite a lot, so put them in a large enough bowl. Relax, beat slowly, and in around 10 minutes you'll have the right density of foam: firm but sinuous. Combine the whites with the béchamel in four stages, with wide movements from the top to the bottom, to avoid breaking the mixture down. It shouldn't be perfectly homogenous... let me explain: it's better to have little clouds of foam rather than working the mixture too hard and risk breaking the whole composition down.

6. Now fill the moulds, up to 2 cm/just under an inch from the edge. Use a spoon, and be careful not to drop the mixture on the edges (remember my previous point about fingermarks? The same thing goes for drops of mixture).

7. Put them in a heat-resistant container: a biscuit tin is ideal. If you use a casserole dish, pour in 2 cm/just under an inch of boiling water before putting in the oven.

8. The cooking time depends on the size. For moulds of 7 cm/just under 3 inches in diameter, 15 minutes will be enough, but for single portion moulds of 10 cm/4" you'll need to allow 20 minutes. In any case, stay nearby, as watching a soufflé rise is an amazing sight, and the only way you can tell it's ready. The dome should be high, golden and without moving bubbles. Remember, too, that an over-cooked soufflé becomes dry... and that would be a shame.

recipes

Fennel and orange salad

In our house, the unbeatable team of fennel and orange is usually accompanied by black olives. Only at Christmas are the tasty dark elements replaced by a hint of red: redcurrants or pomegranates, it doesn't matter which, as long as the dish is full of festive colours!

TIME: 25 MINUTES

SERVES 6

FOR THE SALAD
4 oranges
1 fennel
Redcurrants (or pomegranate seeds)

FOR THE VINAIGRETTE
The juice of 1 orange
2 tablespoons extra-virgin olive oil
1 teaspoon balsamic vinegar
1 tablespoon pomegranate syrup
   (recipe on p.162)
Table salt
Freshly milled black pepper

1. Peel, wash and dice the fennel.

2. Peel the oranges with a sharp knife and slice them.

3. Quickly rinse the redcurrants under cold water and dry with kitchen paper.

4. Prepare the vinaigrette by putting all the ingredients together and beating them with a fork: a vinaigrette worthy of its name must be a really fine emulsion, rather than a liquid with floating oil bubbles.

5. Place the oranges on the serving dish, sprinkle the fennel cubes over the top and pour over the vinaigrette. Add the redcurrants right at the end, because the vinaigrette will spoil them. Serve at once.

❄ *You'll need a sharp knife to peel the oranges. I'm sure you have more than one in your kitchen, but in case you haven't, you should know that keeping your oranges in the fridge an hour before you need them will make the process much easier (the author does not possess even one sharp knife because she is afraid of chopping a finger off). When you cut, start from the North Pole and go down to the South Pole of the orange; this helps you to keep it still as it provides a flat base. Then continue to cut from North to South, with a depth that lets you get to the pulp in one cut. I hope that all these geographical coordinates haven't made your head spin: at least you don't have to make as many cuts as there are time zones… you only need eight.*

Three salads for Father Christmas

When my brother decided that he wanted to work
with horses, he went to Sweden to study veterinary medicine. My
mother went to visit him and came home most enthusiastic. "It's such a
civilised country, there are lots of facilities for couples with children and lovely
shops with furniture kits. But I didn't like their salads. They sell them in jars, as if
they were petunias: my poor boy won't last long there…".
My brother is used to eating vast bowls of salad with every meal and couldn't have it any
other way, so he spent the duration of his Scandinavian stay going back and forth to the
supermarket with trays of plastic jars, each one containing little more than a lettuce leaf. Soon his
house had become an allotment…
Our mother came home with the idea that to create a salad that would be up to her son's standards was
the equivalent of planting a complete vegetable garden.
He came home a year later, but not because of the salads; he settled and put down roots on the top of a hill with
his family, with a vegetable patch in a corner of the garden.
I couldn't help but think about this story when I put these three recipes one after the other. Inspired by Nordic
tradition, they are quite different from our idea of salad: crunchy mixes of various leaves combined and rigorously
seasoned just before being served. You could describe them as salads in a jar: not the aforementioned plastic Swedish
ones for lettuces, but salads you must prepare in advance and keep in the fridge in glass jars. They are very simple to
prepare and great for last minute buffets and aperitifs. Serve them with black bread (sapa bread is perfect) and salted
butter. And don't forget to prepare one for Father Christmas!

Danish-style red cabbage

You'll need a little patience to chop the cabbage into a mountain of thin strips: end of story. It's one of those simple but special recipes that do all the work themselves and are always useful when you're incredibly busy. A large jar of pickled red cabbage in the fridge guarantees you a vaguely exotic side dish (several degrees below zero, given the recipe's origin) that can be ready in a flash: serve it cold, as you would a cucumber salad, or hot with bollito *or roast pork. If you want it to have more of an antipasto feel in a buffet, put it into single portion bowls with a little topping of sour cream.*

TIME: 1 HOUR 15 MINUTES

MAKES ONE 1 1/4 FL OZ JAR

200 ml/6.5 fl oz freshly squeezed
   pomegranate juice (1 big
   pomegranate)
½ red cabbage (about 500 g/1 lb)
2 large shallots
150 ml/5 fl oz cider vinegar
40 g/just under 2 oz caster sugar
   (4 tablespoons)
Table salt
2 tablespoons pomegranate syrup
   (recipe on p. 162)

1. Cut the pomegranate in half and squeeze it as you would an orange, getting as much juice as possible. Sieve it and put to one side.

2. Eliminate the core and outer leaves of the cabbage, wash and cut it in half (into two wedges, a ¼ of a cabbage each wedge). Cut it into thin and regular slices: you need to do this calmly and patiently, above all if, like me, you don't have a collection of samurai blades or swords. As this is the only job of the recipe, do your best.
Once avoided the danger of sinking the knife blade into your fingers, the only remaining risk in a head to head with your red cabbage is to end up with fingers as blue as the face of a Saharan Tuareg. You are warned.
Peel and wash the shallots; slice them thinly, too.

3. Put the cabbage and shallots in a pan – ideally a cast-iron casserole pot, if you have one. Add the vinegar and then the pomegranate juice, sprinkle over some sugar and cook over a medium heat without mixing for a minute or two (you need to let the vinegar evaporate). Put the lid on and leave to cook for about 40 minutes, mixing only now and again to avoid the mixture sticking to the pan. It will be difficult to add the correct amount of salt at this stage, so wait until the cabbage has reduced in volume significantly.

4. When the cabbage is cooked (make sure it's still crunchy; mushy veg is a crime) add the salt. Off the heat, add 2 tablespoons pomegranate syrup if you have some in the fridge (if not, this is a good opportunity to try out the recipe on p. 162); it will melt with the heat from the cabbage. Mix and transfer at once to a spotlessly clean jar.

5. Keep it in the fridge, making sure that the marinade always covers the cabbage. It will keep for two weeks.

Marinated sweet and sour cucumbers

A super-simple, super-quick recipe that you can (in fact, you must) prepare in advance; now, that all sounds appealing, doesn't it? These cucumbers are one of my favourite resources when preparing a buffet, and not just at Christmastime. Always have a jar ready in the fridge, and enjoy finding new companions for them: they work well as a cold salad, alone or with a slice of salmon. They also make a great accompaniment to the classic "black bread, salted butter and anchovy" trio (this is seriously an unbeatable combination…). If they land happily on the top of some blinis with sour cream, they'll feel most at home and very happy. And you'll be happy, too.

TIME: 15 MINUTES + A FEW HOURS RESTING IN THE FRIDGE

MAKES A 500 ML/17 FL OZ JAR

2 cucumbers
2 large (or 3 small) shallots
4 tablespoons cider vinegar
2 tablespoons freshly squeezed lemon juice
3 tablespoons caster sugar
2 teaspoons table salt
Freshly milled black pepper

1. Peel and wash the cucumbers and shallots (if the cucumbers are organic, keep the skin: they're nicer and keep their shape better, too). Slice them as thinly as you can (use a slicer if you have one) and put them in the jar.

2. Add the vinegar and lemon juice, then the sugar, salt and a good sprinkling of pepper.

3. Close the jar and shake it for about ten seconds as if you're making a cocktail (great fun!).

4. Pop the jar in the fridge for a few hours, or, even better, overnight then… let your imagination run free! You can eat these marinated cucumbers in so many ways. You have a week (in the fridge) to experiment.

Marinated apple and herrings

We rarely meet herrings in our part of the world. I'm not referring to out on the high seas, as we all know that the Mediterranean is not the place for herrings, but to the fact that you'll never hear: "Wow, what a lovely herring, I think I'll buy it…" in an Italian fish shop or supermarket, either. We have to hunt for them: in slightly retro grocery stores – the kind where they bring out huge tins of salted anchovies and where they sell olives and capers in brine by weight, or in well-stocked delicatessens with unpopular prices. You might even find them in your local supermarket, hiding behind salmon or smoked tuna, because they sell more of those. That is to say that if you find them, you should be happy, and if you can't manage to find them already filleted, you'll have to do it yourself. It's not difficult, though; even I can manage to do it despite my lack of cutting skills and sharp knives. The only problem when you come face to face with a salted herring is… the smell of herring!

You need to avoid using a wooden chopping board, but use rubber gloves and keep some absorbent kitchen paper handy. But then… let them inebriate you! It doesn't matter if your kitchen ends up smelling like a Baltic fishing boat and someone remarks that, next time, it would be better not to fiddle about with dead fish at teatime: marinated apple and herrings are so delicious. If you make sure that you have some blinis or black bread to hand, this unique salad, as unusual as a Mediterranean herring and which even Father Christmas would love, will be the highlight of your buffets. To eliminate the Baltic fishing boat effect, all you need is ten minutes boiling time – not for the herrings (I mentioned that they don't like warm water), but for the pot-pourri on p. 181: apples, pears, spices, orange peel and the air will soon be filled with the magic of Christmas once more!

Time: 30 minutes + a few hours
resting in the fridge

Makes a 500 ml/17 fl oz jar

100 ml/3.5 fl oz cider vinegar
100 ml/3.5 fl oz water
80 g/just over 3 oz sugar
2 fresh bay leaves
2 juniper berries
8-10 peppercorns
2 herring fillets (60-80 g/
  2 ½-3 ½ oz)
1 red unwaxed apple
1 small leek (about 80 g/
  just over 3 oz after trimming)

1. Put the water, vinegar, sugar, bay leaves, juniper berries and peppercorns into a pan. Bring to the boil over a low heat for a few minutes (the sugar needs to dissolve completely).

2. Cut the herring fillets into little squares or strips small enough for any well-mannered person to eat.

3. Peel the leek and cut it into very fine slices. Wash the unpeeled apple and slice it as thinly as you can (use a slicer if you have one).

4. Put a layer of slightly overlapping apple slices on the bottom of a jar; cover with a layer of leek and then the pieces of herring (it is better not to make this layer too compact, otherwise the herring would be overwhelming). Continue to layer until all the ingredients have been used. Cover with the marinade. This should be cool to avoid cooking the herring (it would be a most inglorious end for a herring to find itself in a jar full of tepid vinegar, having avoided the Mediterranean all its life for fear of warm water!).

5. Put it in the fridge until you are ready to serve: the marinade needs to work its magic for at least 6 hours for the herrings to become completely irresistible. It's a good idea to eat it within a day: it will be fine after that but the apples will break down a little.

❄ *To fillet a salted herring, first you must rinse it under cold water and dry it with kitchen paper. Remove the head, fins and tail, then open it halfway with a cut from the top to the stomach; widen the opening and remove all the innards without breaking the fish up. Eliminate the skin and then look for the bones, which are thin, but long and quite visible. Don't worry if one or two remain, they'll just dissolve, like anchovy bones in the pan.*

recipes

insalata di mele e airuga

Nonnagì's artichoke cream

Nonnagì hates cooking; she does it out of love for others. She has a huge book full of recipes that have become traditional in our family, and if you ask her how to make something, she'll always say: "The recipe says that…", and she'll recite it as if it was straight out of a printed book. "The" printed book, to be precise: the one she keeps on the kitchen shelf. Over the years there has never been a variation, nothing new, not even a slight deviation from the norm; if the book is written clearly and the recipes work, then why change anything? This artichoke cream is one of the rare exceptions, because the recipe isn't printed out on glossy paper, but scribbled in biro on a piece of regularly folded paper, tucked between the pages of the sacred volume, in the chapter "Minestre" (soups). Her friend Natalia gave it to her a long time ago and she has never betrayed it. For fear of altering this timeworn recipe, every time she prepares it out comes the folded piece of paper, which she opens, spreading it out in the palm of her hand, and, raising her glasses above her nose (she says the optician gives her lenses that are unsuitable for reading), she reads out every stage of the recipe line by line. This is exactly what she did when I asked her for the recipe over the phone. I have made one variation though, by using shallots rather than onions. Please don't tell her. I trust your discretion. I don't want her to take me for someone who disrespects tradition, and I want her to keep on reciting bits of paper, so I have an excuse for making modifications.

It's time for me to tell you about her artichoke cream. Here goes: the recipe says…

TIME: ABOUT 2 ½ HOURS

SERVES 4 AS A FIRST COURSE
  OR 8-10 AS A SMALL ENTRÉE

1 small lemon
6 large (or 8 medium) artichokes
2 medium shallots
30 g/just over 1 oz butter
1 tablespoon extra-virgin olive oil
3 tablespoons all-purpose flour
400 ml/13.5 fl oz milk
Vegetable granules
1 extremely fresh egg

❋ *You can prepare this velvety cream the day before. Bring it back to boiling point with a little milk if necessary, before adding the egg.*

1. Prepare a bowl of cold water and squeeze the lemon juice into it. Peel and cut the artichokes into quarters, eliminate the choke and then cut into thin slices (about 8-12 per artichoke). Pop them into the acidic water as soon as you have halved them, while they wait until you have finished their toilette (which must be accurate), to avoid them going brown. If some stalks are tender, leave them on, but be very selective.

2. Peel the shallots, slice them thinly and cook them in a high-sided pan with the butter and oil. Add the well-drained artichokes and allow to absorb the flavour, mixing so that they do not stick to the pan. This step is important: don't burn them, but the later the water is added, the better. If you want your cream to have all the delicate flavour of the artichoke, the last thing you need is burnt or soggy artichokes, so add water only when absolutely necessary, just a little at a time. Cook as you would a risotto, as the artichokes have to be tender.

3. Now pass the artichokes through a mouli, the type your grandmother probably had. There is no technological substitute, hand blender or mixer, for a mouli: the artichoke fibres would escape and hide and then, goodbye cream! With a mouli, you'll be able to separate the fibres from the rest of the artichoke.

4. Put the artichoke purée back into the pan, add first the flour, then, still stirring continuously, add the milk and the vegetable granules. Return to the heat and simmer for 10 minutes (keep whisking).

5. When you are ready to serve, add the slightly beaten egg: whisk briskly to avoid pieces of omelette bobbing about in the cream, which would be most unpleasant…

recipes

Mushroom cream

Shallots and leeks are like dainty stars dancing on points, twirling around with character in the pan and around the house, but never overpowering other ingredients like the troop of Cossacks that is garlic and onions. They prove to be a winning choice every time they form the base of a recipe because they never overwhelm the main ingredient. They are perfect for mushrooms, especially when you replace parsley (another Cossack-style ingredient whose boots risk drowning out any kind of music) with thyme. Once you have tried this variation, it won't be easy to go back: garlic and parsley will end up in other pans, never again with your mushrooms...

TIME: 1½ HOURS

SERVES 4 AS A FIRST COURSE
OR 8-10 AS A SMALL ENTRÉE

30 g/just over 2 oz dried porcini
    mushrooms
1 medium sized leek
1 shallot
20 g/just under 1 oz butter
300 g/12 oz diced potatoes
    (2 large potatoes)
1 fresh bay leaf
4-5 sprigs fresh thyme
300 g/12 oz mixed fresh mushrooms
    (net weight after trimming)
200 ml/6.7 fl oz milk
Vegetable granules
100 ml/just over 3 fl oz fresh cream
Table salt
Freshly milled black pepper

1. Put the dried porcini in a large sieve, rinse quickly under cold water to eliminate any residues of dust or soil, then put them to soak in a bowl of warm water. Don't overdo the rinsing, otherwise you'll remove the flavour, too.

2. Peel and wash the leek, shallot and potatoes; rinse the thyme and bay leaf; rinse the fresh mushrooms in a large sieve.
Thinly slice the leek and the shallot, put them into a heavy-based pan with the butter and make them sweat, stirring from time to time (without burning, keep an eye on them).

3. While a delicious smell begins to pervade your kitchen, dice the potatoes (so that they all cook at the same time as the mushrooms) and throw them in a pan with the bay leaf and the thyme (pull the leaves off, no twigs please).

4. Allow the potatoes to absorb the flavours, stirring often. When there is a risk of sticking, add first the porcini, adding half their soaking water (don't throw away the remaining water!) and then, when the liquid has evaporated, add the fresh mushrooms. They'll produce some vegetable juices in the first few minutes, so add the remaining porcini soaking water only when necessary.

5. Leave to cook over a low heat; when the liquid has dried, add 300 ml/10 fl oz water, the milk and the granules. Continue to cook with the lid on. It will take a maximum of 15-20 minutes: the potatoes should be tender and the mushrooms still whole.

6. Leave to cool, remove the bay leaf, and a porcini mushroom for decoration, and put the rest into the container of a hand blender. Don't overwork it, as the mushroom pieces are really delicious.
Adjust the seasoning, add the cream and serve with a sprinkling of freshly milled pepper. If you have any remaining thyme, add a few leaves to the dishes: they'll provide an unmistakeable aroma...

❄ *As with many vegetable creams, this one can also be prepared a day in advance (which improves it, too!). At point n. 5, put it in the fridge (don't forget the lid) and then start again from point n. 6 the next day, taking care to bring it to the boil for a minute before adding the cream.*

recipes

Borscht

"Turnip head" is no compliment: it is a most unflattering comment for this undervalued vegetable. The turnip, or if you prefer its red variety, beetroot, is the victim of snobbery in Italian kitchens; its qualities are not recognised and it is not very widely used unless in the pre-cooked variety that evokes austere buffets in certain mountain hotels.
I have nothing against pre-cooked beetroot, but if you can find them fresh, bring them home, not only because as soon as you cut them open you'll discover how beautiful they are (I find their colour tone fascinating), but also for all their simplicity.
Borscht is a simple, rustic soup that we have borrowed from the traditions of Eastern European countries. It is good and wholesome, exactly what is needed between one important meal and another during Christmastime.
Just look at that colour… I can think of nothing else in the same league. The pomegranate seeds are optional, but have you ever had a Christmas without baubles, or New Year without pomegranates? This is a great soup.

TIME: 1 HOUR 15 MINUTES

SERVES 4-5 AS A FIRST COURSE
OR 8-10 AS A SMALL ENTRÉE

FOR THE SOUP
500 g/1 lb beetroot net weight after
    trimming (calculate about 650 g/
    1 ½ lb)
2 carrots
1 celery stalk
1 large red onion
1 shallot
1 medium potato
1 red apple
1 tablespoon butter
Vegetable granules
Salt
Freshly milled black pepper

FOR THE FINISHING
Sour cream
Pomegranate seeds

1. Peel and wash all the vegetables and the apple. Slice the shallot and the onion, dice the beetroot and the potato, cut the carrot into thin rounds and the apple into small pieces. Leave the celery whole (or cut it into 2-3 pieces) because you'll have to remove it after cooking.

2. Melt the butter in a heavy-based pan, add the onion and the shallot; sweat for about 5 minutes over a low heat, stirring to avoid them colouring. Add the vegetables and the apple, continuing to stir so that they don't stick to the pan. When they have absorbed the butter, cover with water, add the granules and cook covered until the vegetables become tender (about 30-40 minutes).

3. Reduce to a cream with a hand blender. Add salt and pepper to taste.

4. Serve the borscht with a dollop of sour cream and top with pomegranate seeds. Don't forget a slice of black bread, preferably toasted; it'll be delicious, especially if you spread some salted butter on it.

The apprentice
pasticciere

da guarire
a fa cere...

A few essential tips before you start:

- remove the eggs from the fridge in advance if you can: it will make the whites easier to whip
- an iron whisk is the ideal utensil (with an electric whisk you risk overworking the whites, which won't do)
- both whisk and bowl must be spotlessly clean and without any greasy residues
- the whites must have no trace of yolk, otherwise it'll be impossible for you to get good results on whipping; also, if they are a little stale (by this I mean you've had them in the fridge a while), all the better
- finally: relax! There is absolutely no reason why you cannot produce a wonderful wreath, too

A wreath of meringues

The thought of making meringues frightens many, which is surprising given how easy they are to make. If, like me, you are not willing to give up your good old-fashioned whisk, use Christmas as the perfect opportunity for transforming a few leftover egg whites into a lovely edible wreath.
Meringue will last up to two weeks, so you have plenty of time to think about how you wish to wrap it if you're giving it as a present, or how to fill it if you are keeping it at home. There are infinite options: a meringue base works just as well in a Pavlova as it does for a Montebianco.
If you can't decide which creamy duo to choose: cream and fruit or cream and chestnut, you can always opt for the basic version: a little melted chocolate or a swirl of caramel will be more than sufficient to bring out all the glory of your meringue.

TIME: 1½ HOURS

MAKES A 25 CM/10" DIAMETER
WREATH

4 medium egg whites
110 g/just over 4 oz caster sugar
100 g/4 oz icing sugar

1. Preheat the oven to 120°C/250°F and line a baking tray with parchment paper.

2. Weigh the sugars and put them in two separate bowls. Put the whites in a larger bowl as they will increase in volume.

3. Begin to whisk the whites using large movements, not too fast. After a few minutes a little foam should begin to appear.

4. Only at this stage should you start adding sugar, a little at a time. Begin with the caster sugar, about a quarter of the total amount, and continue to whisk until it has been well incorporated. Keep adding amounts gradually until you have used it all up.
Now it's time for the icing sugar: sift it directly into the bowl (it has an irritating tendency to form lumps, so a sieve is a good idea).
As you proceed, the meringue will become more difficult to work, but don't give up (it's definitely less tiring than walking the dog); collect and add any sugar that sticks to the side of the bowl now and again.

5. Your goal is to obtain a glossy white mixture capable of forming peaks and soft spirals: stop only when you have reached this stage. If you have a little sugar left over, incorporate it with a rubber spatula.

6. Fix the parchment paper to the baking tray with clothing pegs so that it stays still while you make your wreath.
As this is artistic work, you will have your own personal technique.
If you're interested, here's mine: I take small balls of meringue with an ice cream scoop (a spoon is fine, too) and imagining there is a clock face before me, I place a ball at 12 o'clock, one at 6 o'clock, one at 3 o'clock and one at 9 o'clock, in this order (at least for the first two), to make sure they are equidistant. Then I complete the clock face, moving from one number to its opposite number (1 o'clock then 7 o'clock etc). This is how I keep control of the curve. I then use the back of a spoon to create the surface of the wreath with swirls and squiggles – the height of artistic licence… – and the meringue is ready to go in the oven.

7. Bake for 10 minutes with the oven door closed, then open the door by a third and keep baking until it is firm to the touch (about an hour).
Leave to cool with the oven door open and wait a few hours before handling it.

❄ *Four egg whites are quite a lot to whip by hand, so feel free to use an electric whisk if it feels more comfortable. Just be careful not to overwork the whites, otherwise they will look somewhat "scrambled".*

A wreath of cream puffs: profiteroles

You have at least three options for the filling: crème pâtissière, whipped cream or a mix of both. This list is in descending order of density, so you can regulate the filling according to who you think might be eating the profiteroles with their fingers (children…). As far as the decoration is concerned, you can choose: liquid chocolate sauce is great for moistening the profiteroles just before serving, but individual serving dishes are compulsory. A mixture of chocolate and mascarpone (as in the photo) will solidify. This is perfect if you decide that your profiteroles will be eaten with fingers. Both options are absolutely delicious. Now gather the family together and vote for your favourite creamy topping…

TIME: 1 HOUR 45 MINUTES

MAKES 25 PROFITEROLES 5-6 CM/2-2 ½" IN DIAMETER

FOR THE PROFITEROLES
150 ml/5 fl oz milk
150 ml/5 fl oz water
100 g/4 oz butter
A large pinch of table salt
150 g/6 oz all-purpose flour
2 tablespoons vanilla sugar
4 eggs

FOR THE FILLING
300 g/12 oz crème pâtissière (make with: 250 ml/8.5 fl oz milk, 2 egg yolks, 40 g/just under 2 oz sugar, 15 g/½ oz corn starch)
200 g/7 oz freshly whipped cream

TWO FILLING OPTIONS

CHOCOLATE SAUCE
150 g/6 oz dark chocolate (70% cocoa)
50 ml/1.5 fl oz fresh whipping cream
100 ml/just under 3.5 fl oz milk

CHOCOLATE-MASCARPONE GLAZE
200 g/7 oz dark chocolate (70% cocoa)
2 generous tablespoons mascarpone

❄ *If you are a little unsure and you don't quite have the class or the wrist of Audrey Hepburn/Sabrina Fairchild when breaking eggs, do it in advance: put them in a bowl and use a spoon to help you when you have to add them one at a time to the pastry.*

1. Preheat the oven to 180°C/350°F and line a baking tray with parchment paper. Prepare all the ingredients for the choux pastry (let's have fun and call our profiteroles "choux") and keep them nearby.

2. Put the milk, water, butter and salt in a pan and bring to the boil. Just before the liquid rises, take it off the heat and add the flour in one go, mixing vigorously with a spoon. Put it back on the heat for 30 seconds (count…) and keep mixing: you'll have a dense mixture that will gradually resemble a ball. When it comes away from the sides, switch off the hob and add the sugar first, then the eggs, one at a time, mixing continuously. Don't despair if the ball breaks down into pieces after every addition; work even harder and it will return as before.
At the end, the mixture will be smooth, glossy and homogenous – it's very satisfying.

3. Now form the choux, which, as the name suggests, should look a little like cauliflowers. Using two spoons, form little heaps of pastry about 5 cm/2" in diameter. If you like a challenge and you have a reliable oven as well as the right amount in your hands, place the choux on the baking tray in the shape of a wreath; bear in mind that they will rise a little on baking (they blossom like cauliflowers!) and so they'll stick together. Keep a distance between each one of about 1 cm/just under an inch; knowing that no two choux pastries or ovens are the same. You'll have luck on your side as well as a touch of Christmas magic that comes to the aid of even the clumsiest of amateurs.
If, however, you're in a hurry, the day has already been trying enough and you've already used up every ounce of Christmas magic, place little heaps of choux at an orderly distance from each other on the baking tray; you can always make a wreath with them when you are ready to serve (I love plan Bs, and the idea that there is always one…).
If your profiteroles aspire to become Dolomites instead of soft round cauliflowers, smooth out the surface with the spoon.

4. Bake for about 25 minutes. Remove from the oven when they are puffed up and just golden brown. Leave to cool on a cooling rack while you prepare the filling and the decoration.

5. For the chocolate sauce: melt the chocolate, add the warmed milk and cream mixture and combine vigorously. The sauce will be quite a thin liquid initially: you could pop it in the fridge for about 10 minutes, or resign yourself to waiting.
For the chocolate mascarpone decoration: melt the chocolate, add the mascarpone and mix vigorously. Spread on the profiteroles with the back of a spoon.

recipes

The girl from Sarajevo

"You'll be like this tomorrow…" the head nurse told me, slowly lowering the door handle. I tried to focus. In the dim light of the room, a shape connected up to tubes and wires lifted a hand to say hello.
"How's it going, Ajna?"
"Better, thanks…"
"She'll be your roommate from tonight"
Ajna smiled at me.

You'd be wrong to think this is a sad story just because – you got it right – it's set in a hospital. It's actually a story full of cheerfulness, beginning with Ajna and I bursting out laughing the next morning, when a loud speaker crackled with the devotional voice of a nun.
I had slept in an uncomfortable bed; I was labelled "K", followed by an organ name, in my medical record; and I was fully aware that my Christmas holidays – and those of my family, as well – were about to be overwhelmed by a tsunami departing from the surgical unit. Was it really necessary to wake me up at half past five in the morning to praise God from "this valley of tears"?

"Can't they at least keep the volume down?!?" I said, lifting myself up on my elbows. Then I remembered that I wasn't alone in that room, and that different sensibilities must be respected.
"I'm sorry, I don't know what you think, I didn't want to…"
"Oh don't worry! I come from an orthodox family, but I'm a free thinker: in my opinion, a hospital should have good doctors, first. Then, if someone wants him, Our Lord, too"
So, while the nun addressed the ward patients with increasing holy vigour, we got to know each other. I would have lost the opportunity under the influence of a strong anaesthetic a few hours later, so it was worth making the most of the time that the divine broadcast offered us.
Ajna was an architect, educated, a polyglot, young, pretty, temporarily single. She had a job in a prestigious studio, and a new project waiting for her in New York, the following month, if only this problem hadn't cropped up. The same had happened to me, which was why I found myself in her company.

Just so you know, I'm not trying to sugarcoat the story. I was absolutely furious with that monster who had invaded my body completely uninvited. So, if that morning I was looking for a way to wash my hair, it was certainly not with the intention of looking pretty for him.
"À la guerre comme à la guerre" was my motto, and you go to battle wearing uniform, not a pair of slippers.
It was Ajna who told me where to find a shower reserved for staff. "If they find you while you're having a shower, what can they do? Hurry, though, if someone comes looking for you, I'll invent something…"

It was one of the most adventurous showers of my entire life (it would seem that not all patients worry about

stories

134

their hairdo just when the anaesthetist is hunting for them), but this was only the first of many gifts she give me. The greatest one was being, Ajna, a girl from Sarajevo who watched images of her city under siege on TV news. She often spoke to her family on the phone, but she hadn't told anybody what was happening to her. One day her mother asked her why her voice was a little different, and she pretended to have 'flu.

When she explained to me that she lived alone, I was worried: "Ajna, you can't manage alone, the treatments are going to be harsh, you need someone to look after you…"
She pronounced the words slowly, so that even those who refuse to understand have no excuse… "My sister takes her children to school with snipers on the roof. Do you really think it should be me asking for help?"

One good thing – if that's at all possible – about a hospital bed is that you can't just get up and leave: you have to move through words, to find a lighter topic, and we were very good at that. We went into subjects as heavy as boulders, but a moment later we would laugh again. We tried to make the most of any available modicum of happiness. After all, whatever the situation, you should always season your life with a pinch of joy… They let her out on Christmas Eve. We said goodbye like two old friends, but we were not: we'd only known each other four days. She left a drawing on my notebook, with her best wishes and phone number. "And we'll both get over this, ok?"

The surgical unit emptied, they would have closed it for a few days if it hadn't been for me.
"You're the same age as my daughter" the head physician had told me, explaining that he would reopen the operating theatre. So he called back the chief resident from his holidays and saved me. But I, too – in my own little way – made a rescue. "You have rescued me from a holiday with my mother-in-law, dear lady!" repeated the chief resident, whose name was Ambrogio and who was a jolly type. "I am infinitely grateful. It's the first time in twenty years of marriage!" and raised his fist in triumph, with a satisfied smile.

"Oh good! So let's see if you can get me back on my feet as soon as possible. I deserve it now, don't I?"
Spending the holidays like this is not the worst thing that can happen: I had the whole unit to myself, doctors to chat with, nurses who gave me all their attention, as well as the Christmas tree with all its lights. They even prepared a Christmas lunch for me, forgetting that I couldn't eat. My husband did it, on my behalf.

"I've got to go and have lunch with my parents! I can't possibly eat all of this…"
"Oh do be kind, I can't let the cook see all that effort go to waste. Look what a work of art it is! Even olives on slices of *prosciutto*! Go on, you can do it…"
I had tubes coming out of every part of me, as well as the prospect of starting the new year with a substantial dose of chemotherapy, but I kept thinking that it was far more preferable than crossing a road with a sniper on the roof. All thanks to that girl…

As far as Ajna's two wars were concerned, the first to end was the one in Sarajevo; the siege ended two months later. Our personal wars ended later, both victorious. We have never met up again, but we get in touch now and then. We have put the hardest parts of our adventure behind us: it's amazing how you can manage to reset the hard disk of memories. The last time we asked each other what would remain, in another twenty years, of those days together, and we had no doubt: the laughs, our desire for frivolity and lightheartedness. And yes, the memory of a very special Christmas…

Signora Lena's Christmas log

Signora Lena spent her summer afternoons on the terrace, sitting in a wicker chair before a sea the same colour as her eyes. She was an older lady, always very elegant, the kind of elegance that signifies a creative person, never dull. She always wore a touch of colour, a little hint of gold or silver, or a jewel on her outfit and never had a hair out of place. When I passed her garden, I would pay her compliments; she invited them and I paid them sincerely. "You're so full of compliments!", she would remark. "You know, if you want to be with young people you should always look good. If old people don't take care of themselves, they really do get old…". She was as far from being old as you could imagine, with a tribe of grandchildren who adored her. And she smiled. This recipe is hers; I'm happy that it's here, and not only because it's delicious!

TIME: 1 HOUR

FOR THE COCOA SPONGE
5 large eggs
100 g/4 oz caster sugar
60 g/just over 2 oz unsweetened
   cocoa powder
A pinch of table salt

FOR THE FILLING
300 g/6 oz mascarpone
5-6 tablespoons fresh whipping
   cream

FOR THE FINISHING
Icing sugar
A few red berries of your choice

❄ *When rolling up the sponge, begin by pulling the parchment paper behind it, too, and remove it carefully only when you can't go any further. Make sure that the roll is closed well before continuing.*

1. Preheat the oven to 170°C/340°F and line a baking tray with parchment paper (fix the edges with clothing pegs to keep it in place while you spread out the mixture).

2. Separate the eggs and beat the yolks with the sugar until they puff up, become foamy and almost white. Then whisk the whites with the salt until they are like firm snow: don't overdo the whisking, otherwise the whites will appear scrambled.

3. Add the cocoa to the yolks, a couple of spoons at a time, using a sieve to sift it, then mix with wide movements from bottom to top. When you have added about a quarter, begin adding the whites and add a quarter at a time using the same mixing technique to maintain the composition. Alternate the addition of cocoa and whites, until you have the consistency of shaving foam (edible, though…).

4. Pour onto the baking tray and carefully spread it out in a uniform layer, about 1 cm/½" thick (if it's any thicker, you won't be able to roll it without it breaking). If it doesn't completely reach the whole area of the baking tray, it's better to leave a space: you need to create a rectangle.

5. Bake in the oven and stay nearby; sponge cake cooks in 7-12 minutes (depending on your own oven). You'll know it's ready when it puffs up but it's still a little rubbery and soft to the touch (you can touch it when you no longer see moving bubbles on the surface).

6. In the meantime, mix the mascarpone with the cream. On a worktop, spread out a clean damp tea towel that you have rinsed in cold water and thoroughly wrung out.

7. When the sponge cake is ready, remove it from the oven, lifting it on its paper. Allow to dry on a cooling rack (if you don't have one, take it for a walk around the house on its paper). This is a crucial stage; if it becomes too cool, it will lose its elasticity, but if it's still too hot the mascarpone will melt. You need to regulate its temperature well; as soon as you feel it will withstand a lovely spreading of cream without any possibility of melting, transfer it to the damp tea towel and proceed.

8. Spread the mascarpone delicately, to avoid the base crumbling; you should spread it to within 2 cm/just under an inch from the edges. Be quick; every second counts when producing the perfect result.

9. Now breathe deeply because it's the final leg. Very carefully roll the sponge cake (you can do it! See the note on the left) and form the log.

10. Seal with cling film (including the dish) and pop it in the fridge. When you are ready to serve, dust with icing sugar and decorate with red berries.

recipes

Latte brûlé

Don't confuse this with a crème caramel, because you'd be way off the mark. This is a dessert that is not very sweet, just how I like them. There is sugar but it is caramelised and the cream is in its natural state; not sickly at all, so you can serve it even at the end of a special meal. Being super-easy, I've prepared it since I was a child, but in those days, my mother's recipe required a much more generous helping of eggs. Over the years I've gradually reduced this with the result being a finer, more delicate milk brûlé... even my grandmother loves it; she usually wouldn't touch a dessert that wasn't sweet, but this is an exception. My friend Laure adores it too, and she loathes crème caramel. It has quite a fan club, which is still open to new enrolments!

TIME: 2 HOURS 15 MINUTES

FILLS A MOULD OF 23 CM/9"
    IN DIAMETER (FOR 10-12 PEOPLE)

FOR THE PUDDING
1 litre/34 fl oz full cream milk
120 g/just under 5 oz caster sugar
4 egg yolks and 1 whole egg

FOR THE FINISHING
250 ml/8.5 fl oz fresh whipping
    cream

1. Put the milk in a high-sided pan, add 1 tablespoon sugar taken from the total amount and bring to the boil. Lower the heat and leave to simmer for 10 minutes (the high sides should help to prevent any liquid escaping, but stay nearby just in case).

2. Preheat the oven to 180°C/350°F.

3. Prepare the caramel with the rest of the sugar. Put it in a small pan on the smallest hob ring over the lowest heat. Leave it undisturbed until all the sugar has dissolved and it has a good colour... caramel to be precise.

4. Put about ²/₅ of the caramel into the mould. Be extremely careful, as a metal mould will heat up instantly on contact with the boiling caramel! Use oven mitts and try to be as precise as possible: don't pour directly onto the bottom of the mould, but let it run down the sides, tipping the mould slightly as you go. Be as quick as you can because it will solidify rapidly.

5. When you have finished, dilute the remaining caramel in the boiling milk. Fill the caramel pan with milk and wait for it to melt (don't put it back on the heat), mixing from time to time. Keep going until the pan is completely clean and the caramel has been totally absorbed into the milk.

6. Put 4 egg yolks and 1 whole egg into a small bowl and whisk them (use a fork, if you don't have a whisk; but be sure to get yourself one as soon as you can, because you'll need one if you decide to keep following the recipes in this book). When the caramel milk is just warm, pour in the eggs and whisk really well to get a homogenous mixture. Pass through a sieve, and pour into the mould.

7. Cook in a *bain-marie*, until you can insert a knife and it comes out clean without a trace of cream (it'll take about an hour, or an hour and a half, depending on your oven). If the surface begins to colour too much, cover with foil. Once it is ready, leave to cool and put it in the fridge for at least 6 hours (overnight is ideal), sealed with cling film.

8. Before turning it out, run a knife around the edge, then cover with the serving dish and turn it upside down at once; the pudding will emerge in the space of a few seconds, accompanied by the caramel. Whip the cream without adding sugar and decorate your milk brûlé.

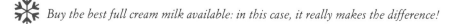 *Buy the best full cream milk available: in this case, it really makes the difference!*

Extra-simple coffee parfait

A minimalist parfait makes life simple, above all when you're busy with other Christmas activities. This one is ready in 10 minutes, and needs only a brief spell in the oven and then in the fridge for it to be perfect. A topping of cream and chocolate curls completes this work of art. If you want to make it for children, you can replace the coffee with instant barley (check which quantities are suitable) and even the youngest can have a grown-up pudding! If the number of guests is much higher than the quantities of ingredients below, you can easily multiply the amounts without compromising a good result. And if you have a problem with containers, don't worry, just take a look at the photo and you'll recognise a glass candlestick, which costs no more than a few cents…
I'm sure that certain recipe books require much more elegant homewares, but this really does work!

TIME: 1 HOUR + RESTING IN THE
FRIDGE

SERVES 4-5 PEOPLE

FOR THE CREAM
200 ml/6.7 fl oz fresh whipping
cream
3 heaped teaspoons instant coffee
2 large egg yolks
3 tablespoons caster sugar

FOR THE FINISHING
100 ml/3.5 fl oz fresh whipping
cream
¼ tablet dark chocolate

1. Preheat the oven to 160°C/320°F and prepare an oven dish that can hold the small glasses of parfait.

2. Warm the cream in a small pan, bring it almost to the boil then remove from the heat immediately. Add the instant coffee and mix well to dissolve. Leave to cool.

3. Whisk the egg yolks with the sugar until they become clear and foamy. Add the cream in a stream and mix delicately (be careful that the cream isn't hot, otherwise both you and the egg yolks will go crazy).

4. Pour the mixture into the small glasses, taking care not to let it drip (drops burn in the oven). Put them in the oven dish, fill it with boiling water and bake for 15-20 minutes.

5. Allow the parfaits to cool before putting them in the fridge, sealed well with cling film, for a few hours (or a whole day if you prefer).

6. Just before serving, decorate with freshly whipped cream and some grated chocolate.

❄ *The quantity of cream that you need for the decoration of the parfait (if you decide not to double the doses) is minimal; you won't manage to whip it with an electric whisk. Resign yourself to using a whisk as it'll only take 5 minutes. Remember to keep the cream in the fridge until the last minute, and if there is enough space, you can also keep the bowl that you'll be using to whip it in the fridge as well: it will make things easier.*

recipes

Jolly
beneficial tipples

Lino and Carmen

I would never have noticed him if I hadn't gone to the bookshop twice a week. It often took ages for our books to arrive, the deliveries were on Tuesdays and Fridays, so with the excuse that the shop assistants were nice, if a little absent-minded, I patiently continued going back. The information desk in the Philosophy section was in a remote corner of the shop - only my husband would want to buy a facsimile of "Dialogue Concerning the Two Chief World Systems" - so I had to hunt for a shop assistant down a long corridor, between ordered shelves of illustrated books: Art and Design on the left, Eroticism and Gay Culture on the right.

I always wondered who had decided that it was necessary to pass through Art and Love to find Galileo and St. Augustine; then I looked over at the occupants of the elegant armchairs, one in every alcove along the corridor, and I came to the conclusion that they weren't there for scholarly purposes. Many of them, bent over photos that were certainly artistic but unmistakable, looked like snooping cowards, in the sense that none of them would have even dared to take one of those books home. You could easily distinguish the people who would buy them: they did not hide and were standing up, usually with a boyfriend by their side. So, as I neared my destination, I thought that this was really a "niche" section, but not only in a metaphorical sense given that, apart from minor philosophers and chic designers, there were people who needed privacy to peek through the pages.

The last alcove, between tomes of Eros and Thought, was inhabited by a rucksack. Given the circumstances, you would have easily thought that the most pusillanimous of all those surreptitious readers had become such a slave to his fears as to have hidden himself inside it, if there hadn't been a man always sitting next to it. With a book in his hand. He was different from the others: he wasn't wearing an elegant architect's baggy jacket, or a skin-tight t-shirt over bronzed muscles. Neither was he flicking furtively through the pages of illustrated books. He was reading books with only words inside, from which I deduced that he would bring them there from another section of that enormous bookshop.

It became clear one day, when I couldn't find the shop assistant at the end of the corridor. I was about to leave when the man who shared his armchair with a rucksack kindly spoke to me.
"He's gone to the stockroom. If you like I'll go and call him…"
"Thank you, but please don't worry. If I know he's in, I'll wait"
"I would. Your books are there!" and he pointed to a shelf behind the counter.
There were the two volumes I had been waiting for, but his certainty disorientated me. I would have defined it professionalism, if he wasn't lacking some tangible sign of the profession: he wasn't wearing a uniform, he didn't have a name badge, neither did he have that air of impatience of many shop assistants when they're waiting for their shift to end so that they can go home. Quite the opposite.

stories

144

My favourite shop assistant had a crown of Rasta plaits on top of his head, tattooed arms that hung out of baggy t-shirts, and an intelligent face. According to his badge, his name was Tommaso.

"If it hadn't been for this man, I would have left…" I told him when he reappeared.

"Well, we couldn't do without Lino, either!" he replied. Lino – no longer just the man with the rucksack – smiled.

A few days later I was back in the bookshop once again, tied up with other orders and titles. He was there, too, in the last armchair in the corridor after the other occupied alcoves. Of course, the shop assistant was nowhere to be seen.

"Good morning, Signora!"

"Good morning! Is Tommaso always in the stockroom? I think it would be quicker to ask you…"

There was a moment of slight embarrassment.

"If it was up to me, I would help you, but I can't be seen doing such things… The boys help me out but the less I am seen the better it is, for them, too"

"Oh, I'm sorry. I had thought you were…"

To be honest, I didn't know myself who I thought he was. I'd never really thought about it.

It was up to him to tell me.

"I… well, let's say I live here. During the day… because at night I go to the shelter, but I'm here in the day, so that I'm not on the streets…"

In my own limited database of available expressions, none of them would have been suitable.

"I'm homeless, Signora. I lost my job… I had a few debts, and everything went wrong, I didn't even realise it myself. I came to the city where no-one knows me. But I refuse to be on the streets, there are all types out there and I don't want to be like them. I've still got my dignity…"

At that moment, Tommaso Crown-of-Rasta-Plaits arrived. One look was enough.

"Have you seen what a force of nature our Lino is? He's a great warehouseman! In case you need one…"

But what could a lady do with a warehouseman? Nothing, absolutely nothing and even Lino knew it. I couldn't do anything else but being silent. Moreover, I wouldn't have known what to say.

"Please, act as if you don't know a thing…" he said, winking. "So far the manager has pretended not to notice, but if they find out then both of us will lose our jobs… and then Lino, well, he'll become a tramp!" and he started to joke with his friend.

It wasn't a sad scene, far from it. There was a lot of empathy, affection, even cheerfulness in their making fun of each other, and although you won't believe it, Lino was the one who smiled more than all of us. Of course, my books had not arrived…

I went behind the cash desk. "Listen, Tommaso" (now that I knew his secret, I could call him by his first name) "I'd like to buy a book for that man, can you recommend something?"

He looked at me with the expression of someone who wants to tell you that actually you haven't understood a thing, but doesn't want to upset you. "I wouldn't know, he reads so many here, and I don't think he'd even know where to carry one"

Hit and sunk. It's not as if you need a great deal of intuition to understand that giving a book to someone who has a rucksack for a home is a little like giving a floor lamp to a sailor leaving for a solo transatlantic voyage. I had just done one of those stupid things that some charitable women do, and that I absolutely loathe. I felt totally inadequate. Of course, I knew such situations existed, but when you actually come across them and they have a name, eyes, words and even books in their hands, well, it's altogether a different story.

I went on holiday and my thoughts often turned to Lino, with only those bookshelves to call home. It was September when I came back, and this time my books were there, along with the sneaky readers of spicy volumes. But I could not help but notice one empty armchair…
"Where's Lino?" I asked Tommaso Crown-of-Rasta-Plaits even before greeting him.
"Well, great news… he's found love!"
"Really?! Where?"
"Where do you think he found it, being stuck in here all day?" and raising his voice, he added: "Carmen arrived and took him… isn't that right, Carmencita?" and he looked past a metal trolley overloaded with trembling towers of books, which was moving towards us like as if it was propelled by a misterious force. A couple of seconds and the poltergeist revealed her identity: Carmen, affectionately known as Carmencita, a profile as sharp as the stones of Cusco walls, barely a metre and a half in height, and a waistline the same length as Cordillera. She had a long jet black plait and wore the red shop uniform: this time no-one risked losing their job.

"This is Lino's fiancée…" said the shop assistant, bowing to Carmencita.
"Hoy, Tommaso! No more shokes!" she said, swatting an inexistent fly. Her Andean face had lit up.
"But I no shoking! So where is the champ today?"
"With Don Gino, a pintar the oratory…"
"But then you'll get home tonight he'll have cooked dinner for you… Signora, did you know that Lino's a great chef?"
Carmen threw back her head with a crystal laugh, pointing to her generous hips. Then placed two piles of books on the table and disappeared with her trolley back through the shop.

"I'm going home a happier woman this evening, you know? And not just for the books"
"We're happy, too, Signora, for Lino and for Carmen. Before Lino, she was with a guy who was a danger to the public…"
"What kind of danger?"
"The kind that ends up in jail, every now and again. But this time he'll be there for quite a while. Even the vicar, when he found out, said: 'God sees all and will provide'. And now Lino is assisted by the parish, too. He lives with Carmen and her sister with two children, but she has a salary. They'll manage"

I would have liked him to tell me that story again. It was so lovely that it was perfect: there was no need to add another word. A book, though, yes.
"I think the time has come to choose that famous book, do you remember? The one you didn't want to sell me two months ago. You can choose it, and I'll write a dedication"
He came back with "Around the World in 80 Days", because Lino loved adventure stories and conceptual titles wouldn't have been appropriate.

stories

146

More weeks and books came and went, as well as chatters with my favourite shop assistant who, in the meantime, had had his hair cut short, so I could only call him Tommaso, seeing that he no longer had his Rasta plaits. We had become friends, thanks to Lino. He told me that the romance with Carmen continued, that Lino was still out of work but from time to time he found something to do, and he'd also learned Peruvian cooking. There was the parish church, the local social club, so they weren't lonely. As far as me, I'd got into the habit of reading any local news that had the word "gang" or "pandilla" written in the headlines, have you ever seen them? I worried that they might let the public danger out early, and to celebrate he'd go and find Lino. Thankfully, there was nothing like that in the newspaper.

A year passed.

It was December when, coming out of the cinema late one evening, I found myself in front of the bookshop. It was closed but inside there was a to-ing and fro-ing of busy people, putting up new shelves and decorating the windows for Christmas.

"Must you stop and window-shop in this freezing cold?" my husband moaned. "And look, they're working, you'll bother them, there's a chap knocking on the glass, you need to move…"
Of course I needed to move! Lino couldn't get near the window while the panels were in the way. He greeted me from behind the glass and, if my lip-reading was any good, he thanked me, while turning the pages of a book only he and I could see.
"What are you still doing here?" I asked, gesturing eloquently with my hands. He was the only one without a uniform, it was clear he was… let's say a helping guest. He pointed to a mountain of boxes: Carmen, known affectionately as Carmencita, stock room manageress, peruana, was opening cartons of books with her Andean aplomb. He, with the others' evident complicity, was helping her.
Then he made a universally understood gesture with his hand. So I lowered my eyes to where Carmen's plait fell, and saw that her Cordillera-waist had a new peak: one of the kind that you can only name once you've found out if it's pink or blue.
Trembling with cold, we briskly walked home. A thick fog wrapped itself around the half-deserted city. The fairy lights seemed like milky drops expanding in the air.
"Brrr… I'm absolutely freezing. You manage to find all sorts, you do! Who were they?!?"
"Do you remember when I went to collect your books? I met them then"
"They didn't look much like booksellers to me…"
"And who told you that they were?"
"The cold is making you crabby. And look… there's a drop under your left eye"
"Oh, it's just the rain…"
"I'd like to inform you that it's not raining, but never mind. For a moment I thought it was all about those two…"
"The stories you come up with! Look how lovely that building is, with its Christmas lights…"

Irish coffee I love you

This is the only concoction with a hard liqueur base that I could ever drink when I was young and I have great memories about it. It's a shame to drink it alone, so you need to make enough for at least two. Of course, you can always multiply the quantities…

TIME: 20 MINUTES

SERVES 2

50 ml/just over 1 ½ fl oz cream
2 tablespoons muscovado sugar (or other cane sugar)
2 tablespoons water
200 ml/6.7 fl oz boiling coffee, freshly made in a moka pot
50 ml/just over 1 ½ fl oz whisky (the best you can afford)
Nutmeg

1. Whip the cream with a whisk. It shouldn't get too firm, so it'll only take a moment. Stop as soon as you see that the bubbles have disappeared and you can draw swirls. Put it in the fridge (sealed!) until you are ready to serve.

2. Fill some glasses with very hot water (this is obviously not the water you'll use for the recipe).

3. Put the sugar and water in a pan over a low heat. Dissolve the sugar, mix and switch off the heat as soon as the liquid takes on a syrupy consistency (it'll be ready in two minutes).

4. Prepare the coffee and enjoy the sound of it rising from the moka pot – blob, blob, blob – with the delicious aroma wafting around the kitchen. While you're there, you can wonder at the fact that coffee made in a moka pot is now a pleasure for only a few snobs: relish every drop of it.

5. As soon as the coffee has risen, empty the glasses and pour in (in this order): the syrup, the whisky and then the coffee, up to two centimetres/just under an inch from the rim.

6. Bring the cream out of the fridge. Take a spoon and use it to drop the cream into the glasses. Stop when it reaches a few millimetres/barely ¼" from the rim.

7. Grate a little nutmeg into each glass and… savour the moment!

❄ *The sugar syrup is a little touch of class; it's delicious, especially when the glass begins to empty and the remaining coffee gradually becomes sweeter. It makes your Irish coffee experience unique for as long as it lasts, and adds texture to the coffee, making it denser. I recommend that you include this element, but if you don't feel like getting another pan out, divide the quantity of sugar between two glasses, pour in the whisky, mix and then proceed with the rest. Do not to omit the sugar syrup next time you make this, though…*

recipes

Golden rules for making the perfect Irish coffee

COFFEE – Make it in a coffee pot: no filters, capsules or other similar devices. The perfect concentration for our latitudes, is that of a coffee freshly made in a vintage Bialetti moka pot (I know that in Ireland, vintage Bialettis are not so common, but that's, in fact, quite a way from our Italian latitudes).

SUGAR – It is absolutely essential, so you can't think of leaving it out (an Irish coffee without sugar is like cheese without fat; it would be an unspeakable mistake and extremely revolting).
I would add here, if I haven't already managed to convince you, that if the liquid isn't sweet, the cream won't float. I hope I have frightened you enough.

CANE SUGAR – Demerara, muscovado, soft brown sugar or whatever you prefer, it must be cane sugar. The more aromatic it is, the better. So use the sugar that you like or that you have to hand.

TEMPERATURE – Hot glasses, boiling coffee, really cold cream; this is the formula. To ensure all this, you need to warm the glasses in advance with boiling water, make fresh coffee, whip the cream in advance and keep it in the fridge until it's needed.

CREAM – Use only fresh whipping cream, and this applies not only to Irish coffee, but also for every other edible situation; spray cans are only for shaving foam. So, please use only freshly whipped cream (reserve your curls and artistic licence for Saint Honoré puddings).
When you are there with the aroma of whisky and coffee coming up from the glasses, play the spoon game: hold a spoon under hot water for a few seconds, dry it, turn it and let the cream slide down the back of it while you draw a circle inside the glass. Stop when the cream is 1 cm (to be precise, half an inch) thick and near to the rim of the glass.

THE GLASS – A heavy glass, with a stem (a handle is optional). Test the glass if you're not sure it can withstand the heat (a series of exploding glasses full of hot coffee is not exactly what one would expect during a peaceful Christmas evening). Try it with water straight out of the kettle, before destroying the entire family glass collection. Regarding the stem, it's not just an aesthetic point – you try holding a glass at high temperature…

Hen's milk

Glasses that are destined to host a so-called "spirit" are never all the same. They widen or narrow according to our perception. I can't handle hard liquor, so I tend to keep the bar low; for this reason I've written the quantities below as "extendable", especially for rum. Now, you should know that I'm quite an expert in extendable glasses, more than hard liquor, because our mother made us keep one in our school bag when we were at elementary school. It was like a set of pocket binoculars, made of concentric glasses, which lengthened or shortened depending how thirsty we were. And it had a screw top. The aim of having it was for us to avoid drinking directly from the tap, like our friends did; whether out of sheer contempt for danger or maintaining a safe distance, all the children in our school drank from the toilet tap when they were thirsty (they were wonderfully spartan times).

Everyone except for us. To compensate, on hot summer afternoons running around the vegetable garden, we would drink from the rubber hose that Gambucci left on the ground. We scraped off the crusts of mud before turning on the tap and then we savoured our transgression right up to the last drop. Now that I think about it, maybe there was even a touch of fertiliser in that mud, the kind that would nudge up the price of vegetables, today being organic. From another point of view, we probably ingested a certain amount of cow's fecal bacteria along with the water. No-one ever ended up in hospital, our mother never found out and that water was worth much more than a Coca Cola to us. It wasn't as if it were of unknown origin; it came from Gambucci's cows…

TIME: 20 MINUTES

SERVES 8-10

750 ml/25 ½ fl oz full cream milk (the best you can find)
250 ml/8.4 fl oz fresh whipping cream
4 cinnamon sticks of about 6 cm/ 2.3"
1 vanilla pod
8 tablespoons brown cane sugar (60-80 g/just over 2-3 oz, depending on your spoons and your inclination for sweetness)
4 yolks from super-fresh eggs and happy hens
1 small glass of rum (between 50 and 100 ml/1.7- just under 3 ½ fl oz)

TO SERVE
100 ml/just under 3 ½ fl oz fresh whipping cream
Powdered cinnamon

1. Whip the cream and put it in the fridge covered with cling film.

2. Put the milk, cream and cinnamon sticks in a small pan.

3. Open the vanilla pod, remove the seeds with the tip of a knife and add them to the mix of cream and milk. Put the empty pod in as well; it won't go into your glasses, but you should do all you can to get as much of its wonderful aroma.

4. Warm the mixture over a medium heat; switch off the hob ring as soon as you see it begin to tremble, because it mustn't boil.

5. Whisk the egg yolks with the sugar. When they are clear and foamy, add the rum and whisk again.

6. Remove the vanilla pod, using your fingers to squeeze any liquid out along its length, then pour the milk in a stream onto the egg yolk and sugar, whisking. Filter the mixture (a fine sieve is all you need), pour into the glasses and decorate with a spoonful of whipped cream and a dusting of cinnamon powder.

❄ *If, while you're whisking the egg yolks with the sugar, the milk begins to cool, pop it back on the heat and bring it almost to the boil; this hen's milk should be nice and hot, if you want to smell the aroma of vanilla melt deliciously with the sugar and rum. Be careful that it doesn't become "too" hot, otherwise when you pour it onto the eggs you'll risk producing unpleasant lumps. So make sure it's hot but not boiling, and keep on whisking while you pour it in a stream over the eggs. And if you're anything like me, whenever you use eggs, and you don't want to risk chalazae (those abominable blobs that are only useful for a chick and not when you're going to eat the egg) turning up in your dish, remember to strain the mixture. You've been warned…*

The way to make mulled wine syrup

The quickest way to make mulled wine – very useful if you are overcome with the desire for it, or your friends suddenly turn up, as well as being a great Christmas gift – is to make a syrup. Like all speedy solutions, it needs a preventative stage: the preparation of a syrup, that you should warm with the wine of your choice in these proportions: 1:2,5…?!? Is your head spinning? Let's look at it this way: for a 750 ml/25.3 fl oz bottle of wine, you'll need 300 ml/10 fl oz syrup, so that's one part syrup to 2 ½ parts wine. Now it's time to run to the kitchen, crack open that bottle of Barbera and see if you can make your head spin in other ways.

In case you need an extra kick, please be informed that 75 ml/2.5 fl oz red port will work really well as an optional addition to help you reach your objective. On the other hand, as I don't wish to be taken for someone who encourages others on the road to alcoholic perdition (my mother would not approve it), I must point out that this syrup is completely innocuous, because it contains not even a drop of alcohol. We can now look at ways of modifying the recipe, according to the age of the adventurers. Adults will add it to wine, children to fruit juice, and grandparents… they can decide on the spur of the moment if they belong to the adult or the child world!

TIME: 45 MINUTES

MAKES ABOUT 300 ML/10 FL OZ SYRUP

500 ml/17 fl oz water
150 g/6 oz muscovado sugar
100 g/4 oz caster sugar
The zest of 1 unwaxed lemon
1 unwaxed orange
1 unwaxed mandarin
1 fresh bay leaf
10 cloves
1-2 juniper berries
6 cinnamon sticks of about 6 cm/ 2.3"
4 star anise fruits
5 peppercorns
A piece of fresh ginger

1. Rinse the bay leaf; peel, wash and slice the ginger.
Wash the lemon, orange and the mandarin; remove the zest with a sharp knife. Be careful to keep the orange and mandarin intact, as you need their juice. Squeeze them as you prefer (electric juicer or a good squeeze with your hand).

2. Put the water, sugars, lemon zest, zest and juice of the orange and mandarin, the bay leaf and all the spices into a pan. Boil over a low heat for 20-25 minutes.

3. Filter the syrup through a sieve with fine holes and transfer to a spotlessly clean glass jar. It will keep in the fridge for 2 months.

recipes

Mulled wine for grown-ups...

Now that you have your syrup, here are the quantities for mulled wine, in grown-up version.

TIME: 10 MINUTES

SERVES 8

750 ml/25.3 fl oz red wine (a Barbera
or close relative is perfect)
75 ml/2.5 fl oz port (if you fancy it)
300 ml/10 fl oz mulled wine syrup

TO DECORATE
Orange slices
Cinnamon sticks

1. Put the wine, and the port if using, into an iron or enamel pan (non-stick ones often have a little residual smell that might tarnish this recipe). Add the syrup, mix and bring almost to the boil. Leave to simmer on the lowest heat for a few minutes. In the meantime, wash, dry and slice the orange.

2. Pour your mulled wine into glasses with handles (it should be served boiling hot) and decorate with the cinnamon and orange slices.

... and for the little ones

"Come on children, it's time for mulled wine!". To tell the truth, I have never heard this. However, alcohol aside, there is no reason why the children can't have their little Christmas treat, too.
It doesn't take much; all you need to do is replace the wine with fruit juice, and it's done! You can still add the spicy syrup, citrus slices and cinnamon sticks just like the grown-ups' recipe. It becomes a little lesson in taste, with a competition to guess all the aromas that come out of the glass. Whoever gets the most, wins a second serving.

TIME: 20 MINUTES

SERVES 2

100 ml/3.3 fl oz freshly squeezed
pomegranate juice
100 ml/3.3 fl oz apple juice
1 tablespoon mulled wine syrup

FOR THE FINISHING
Apple pieces
Slices of orange or mandarin
Cinnamon sticks

1. Cut the pomegranates in half and squeeze it using a juicer. If they are very big and you get the impression that the seeds haven't been fully squeezed, transfer them to a sieve and use your hands. Filter the juice.

2. Mix the pomegranate juice with the apple juice in equal parts, adding a good spoonful of mulled wine syrup for every 200 ml/6.7 fl oz juices. Warm in a pan, allow to simmer for a few minutes. Pour it into glasses and decorate with apple pieces, slices of orange and cinnamon sticks. Then call up your troops: "Children, it's time for some mulled wine!".

recipes

Hypocras

Wine, honey and spices are used for this recipe that goes back a long way, to the medieval "dark ages", to be exact. The passing of time has not diminished its charm; it's incredibly easy to make and truly delicious. Hypocras is a sort of predecessor of vermouth, and it's a real pleasure. Serve it cool in small glasses, but it can also be used in jellies, with baked pears, and as a substitute for port in liver pâté (p. 68).
It is important to put the crushed spices in a bag, otherwise they'll mix with the honey and it will be impossible to filter the wine without the help of a spoon, so the Hypocras will turn cloudy.
You can use a scrap of old napkin – fine linen is ideal – or a shirt, or even better, a piece of kitchen gauze, which must be extremely clean and without a trace of perfume (no fabric softener, bleach, starch or similar chemical weapons; in the dark ages they hadn't even been invented).
If you have one of those American coffee filters, you'll be verging on perfection. It doesn't matter if coffee filters didn't exist in medieval times, because coffee was still beyond Hercules' columns together with the Americas…

TIME: 20 MINUTES + 1 NIGHT
OF REST

100 g/4 oz wildflower runny honey
1 bottle still red wine (Merlot for
    example)
about 50 g/2 oz fresh ginger
10 cloves
10 cardamom pods
5 cinnamon sticks of about 6 cm/
    2.3"

1. Prepare a large capacity container. A glass jar, a bowl of earthenware or varnished metal or a jug is fine; make sure it is clean and without a trace of odour (which is why plastic should be avoided). If it has a lid, all the better, otherwise you can cover the opening in some way.

2. Put the honey in a small pan and warm over a very low heat; it mustn't boil, just become more fluid. Remove from the heat, add a little wine and mix until the honey is perfectly diluted. Pour the mixture into your container with the rest of the bottle.

3. Peel, wash and dry the ginger. Slice and add to the wine.

4. Bash the spices coarsely with a meat tenderiser (if you don't have one, use a rolling pin but be careful not to squish your fingers), wrap in a piece of fine cloth, tie it tightly with kitchen string and add to the sweetened wine. The little bag of spices tends to float, so you should weight it down to ensure that no precious spice aromas escape. You don't need an anchor – I just put a spoon on the top of it.

5. Leave to rest for a night (or two), filter through a fine cloth and bottle.

6. Drink Hypocras cool but not iced, so bring it out of the fridge a little in advance of serving. Pour into small glasses (it's still alcoholic, even if sweet), in good company if possible. It will keep in the fridge for 2 months.

❄ *Choose a wildflower honey or any other type with a gentle aroma if you wish your Hypocras to taste of wine, albeit sweet and spiced. Chestnut honey and suchlike can be reserved for other uses.*

sciroppo di melagrana

Syrups & jellies

Pomegranate syrup

A delight, beginning with its colour. It loves being paired with ice cream, panna cotta *and meringues with cream. Divine on toasted bread and butter, it's equally good in a vinaigrette; all you need is a teaspoonful mixed with some balsamic vinegar. It also adds more colour to the Danish red cabbage recipe (p. 115). It makes a scrumptious gift that you can prepare well in advance, and almost everyone loves it. I think you have enough reasons to get started!*

TIME: 1 HOUR 15 MINUTES

MAKES 250 ML/8 ½ FL OZ SYRUP

500 ml/17 fl oz freshly squeezed
   pomegranate juice (about 5-7
   pomegranates)
1 large lemon
250 g/10 oz caster sugar

1. Cut the pomegranates in half and squeeze them with a juicer. If they are very big and you think that the seeds haven't produced all their juice, transfer them to a sieve and use your hands to squeeze them. Don't lose even a drop of their precious juice! It will need to be filtered, using the same sieve.

2. Squeeze the lemon and filter the juice.

3. Put the pomegranate and lemon juice in a small high-sided pan. Add the sugar, mix and boil over a high heat for about 30 minutes. The liquid should reduce by roughly half. The syrup is ready when it is glossy, sticky and dense. It will thicken more on cooling.

4. Pour it into a spotlessly clean jar. Leave to cool uncovered, then close and keep in the fridge. It will last for 2-3 months.

Pear and ginger syrup

This could make up a "Christmas Syrups" duo together with the previous recipe, to give as a gift to your foodie friends. You can decide, depending on who the recipients are, if you want to specify on its label that it goes very well with gin, mixed in variable proportions with fruit juice...

TIME: 1 HOUR 15 MINUTES

MAKES ABOUT 250 ML SYRUP

750 g/26 ½ fl oz unwaxed pears
   that are not too mature
A good-sized piece of fresh ginger
250 g/8.8 fl oz caster sugar
500 ml/17 fl oz water

1. Wash the pears well; peel and wash the ginger. Cut the pears into large pieces without peeling or removing the seeds or core. Slice the ginger.

2. Put everything into a medium thick-bottomed iron pan. Add the sugar and water, then gently boil over a low heat, for 30-35 minutes from boiling point.

3. Filter the syrup through a fine sieve. If you have an iron sieve, even better; place it over a bowl, tip the syrup in and let the pears drip out all their juice. You can press lightly with the back of a spoon to aid the process, but not too much: a cloudy syrup is not a syrup.

4. Pour into a spotlessly clean jar and leave to cool uncovered. Close and keep in the fridge. It will last 2-3 months.

recipes

Mulled wine syrup

Not to be confused with the syrup "for" mulled wine on p.154 with a base of sugar and aromatic spices, this syrup is made of wine, flavoured with spices and citrus fruit, then sweetened as much as you wish. It's a mulled wine reduced to its very essence, made for pouring over an apple tart tatin or panna cotta (can you imagine a more Christmassy version?). Like honey, it will happily accompany a plate of mature cheeses.
Its aroma captures the very essence of Christmas…

TIME: 1 HOUR 15 MINUTES

MAKES 250 ML/8 ½ FL OZ SYRUP

5 cinnamon sticks of about 6 cm/
  2 ½"
10 cardamom pods
3 star anise fruits
10 cloves
10 peppercorns
500 ml/17 fl oz red wine
200 g/6 oz caster sugar
The zest of 1 unwaxed lemon
2 unwaxed mandarins
1 piece of fresh ginger
Nutmeg
1 vanilla pod

1. Put the halved cinnamon sticks, freshly crushed cardamom pods (don't reduce them to a powder: all they need is one bash of a meat tenderiser), peppercorns (crush as for the cardamom), the star anise and cloves into a non-stick pan.

2. Toast the spices for 3-4 minutes, moving the pan continuously to avoid burning. Switch off the heat as soon as you smell the aromas and leave to cool.

3. Wash the lemon and use a sharp knife to peel the zest. Wash the mandarins. Peel, wash and slice the ginger finely.

4. Put the wine and sugar into an iron pan. Add the toasted spices, lemon zest, halved mandarins and the ginger slices.
Grate a little nutmeg directly into the pan (don't be afraid to add more).
Cut the vanilla pod in two, collect the seeds with a knife; put both seeds and pod into the pan.

5. Simmer 20–25 minutes.

6. Remove the mandarins. As soon as you can handle them, squeeze out every last drop of juice and syrup. Do the same with the lemon zest.
Filter the syrup through a fine sieve, then transfer it to a spotlessly clean jar. Keep in the fridge. It will last for 2-3 months.

❄ *Be careful, the spices burn easily. In this recipe, the pieces are of different sizes, so the smaller ones risk burning even more. Remove from the heat as soon as they begin to release their aromas. If you feel that you only just missed carbonising them, don't leave them to cool in the pan, but put them on a plate at once. A cold plate…*

recipes

The little glass bird

"Signora... it won't get through the door!" said Gambucci with a solemn expression, opening his arms wide. A woollen peaked cap in hand, and heavy corduroy trousers with two large greenish puddles at the knees, he respectfully stayed in the doorway, a step back from the threshold, because if he'd gone in with his big muddy boots, Delfina would have threatened him with the broom.
"What do you mean, it won't get through the door?"
"Well, it will, but sideways. We've tried standing it up but it's too tall, it'll touch the ceiling... if you want we'll chop off half a metre..."
"Don't even think about it!" my mother replied indignantly, "We'll have to find another solution."

Pruning the trees was one of Gambucci's obsessions. He tended to solve with draconian cuts the slightest problem might arise in the garden: be it powdery mildew, aphids on the roses, or a bush that he thought was too exhuberant, in his opinion there was never an alternative.
"Let's take up our arms and go!" was his battle cry. He stuck his pipe in the gap where three teeth were missing, swiftly picked up all his tools and set off walking, boldly. Chop! chop! You could hear shortly after, and the fate of the plant that had dared to challenge him was no longer a mystery.
As we knew him so well, we usually managed to prevent him from going too far, by stopping his murderous hand before it sank the garden shears into the latest victim. Once, he had chopped back an entire border of oleander and plumbago to perfection, while we were at the beach, because "crooked bushes are for those poor people". So, for a whole year, we'd got our hedge resembling the central reservation of a motorway, and our father would get cross every time he looked at it, but Gambucci was more than satisfied.

I apologise for my lengthy description, but I had to tell you all of this to help you understand the kind of threat my mother had to cope with. It was a dire situation. It was three o'clock in the afternoon of 23 December: huge clouds billowed in the sky, sending the light beyond the strip of sea on the horizon, and, weather details apart, a tempest was about to hit our Christmas traditions. Unless we considered having a Christmas tree that ended up like one of Gambucci's hedges, the ghost of a Christmas without a tree had slipped into our house, without even knocking. It hung around the living room, stroking the wooden boxes of baubles, wrapping itself around the shiny tinsel that lay over the back of a chair and the two baskets of rolled up tree lights waiting to be draped on branches.

The little glass bird was sitting on the piano in its nest of card, with shredded tissue paper all around it as it was extremely fragile and with children nearby, who knows what might happen... It was a kind of seal, the final touch to our tree-dressing ceremony, along with putting up the star. It was our mother who always placed them both on the tree, up a ladder, and if it was quite easy with the star (she just needed to

stories

166

take extra care as, we all know, you can't shape a real Christmas tree), things got complicated when it was the turn of the glass bird: she always had to settle any disputes before placing it, because it was up to us to choose which branch it should go on.

The living room was still, as if waiting to know if the showing of the film "Natale in Famiglia" would start again – it was always the same film, but the audience loved it. The fireplace crackled, the candles in the candlesticks were all in place, we were all beside ourselves with excitement as school had just finished: fifteen wonderful days of holiday, the most exciting of the whole year, awaited us. However, the great wicker basket, which had been brought up freshly washed from the cellar to hold the pot with the fir tree, was sadly empty. It seemed destined to remain so, if not for a little Gambuccian intervention that didn't even bear thinking about…

Mamma did not lose heart and shortly afterwards we were all in the car. She drove in a pair of low-heeled square-toed patent leather boots (I wish I still had them today, they'd look great!); Delfina, by her side, wearing her men's slippers, a woollen scarf tied under her chin as if she was going for a scooter ride, in her brown coat over her checked uniform (a figurino…); and finally the three of us, sitting behind them, in the lace-up ankle boots we always wore for playing in the garden, with our ski jackets on, because at Christmastime we could even go sledging if our neighbouring farmer thought that there was enough snow to protect his wheat field.

There wasn't a great deal of choice at the garden centre, everyone knows you shouldn't leave it to the last minute if you want a really nice Christmas tree. But our own, which lived in a remote corner at the end of the vegetable garden for 350 days a year, had just betrayed us. It had suddenly become too tall, and after years of distinguished service, it had inexplicably decided it didn't want to get into our house anymore. And who knows what on earth it had in mind, because we had treated it so well… serves it right! Of course, we would never have abandoned it to Gambucci's shears, but from that year on it gained a neighbour that was somewhat hard to get along with.

On the way home, we were a sight to be seen. Three children, a housekeeper and a Christmas tree all inside a tiny Fiat 500 was a real challenge for anyone, least of all for our mother. The tree didn't fit in the boot, so the only way was to squash it inside with us: a very direct but affectionate way of getting to know each other. Delfina carefully allowed it to poke through the sun roof, pushing her own seat forward a little, and told us to close our eyes otherwise we would have had to make a trip to the hospital as well as the garden centre, that day. I don't know if you have ever had to sit in a car right next to a Christmas tree, but in case you haven't had the pleasure, I tell you what happens: it pricks you at every turn, worse than a cactus… And if you are a child and you are told to keep your eyes closed, the feeling of being at the mercy of all around you is even stronger than the excitement of such an adventurous journey. "There's a bend comiiiing!" shouted Mamma, and we stiffened inside our jackets, in a vain attempt to limit the damages.

When we got home, Gambucci brought the newcomer inside. If he was disappointed, he didn't show it: he went back to the vegetable garden, put the old unruly fir tree back in its place and… chop! chop! He consoled himself with a couple of damaged branches.
Meanwhile, there was a hive of activity in the living room: a debate on where to hang the baubles, serious discussions of where to put the tinsel and tree lights (divided into colours? lengthways or widthways?

and so on). Until – one pulls to the right, then the other to the left, and the third, being the cheekiest of all, suddenly yanks some lights from behind – the tree… oooooh!... crash!... with a sound of snapping branches, fell down.

It landed between the piano and the ladder we'd just used to put up the star, with its load of tinsel, lights, arguments, dreams, colours and… baubles. Small shiny shards rocked gently on the floor, while our mother's hard stare went from one of us to another. But there's a time for all things, also for tellings-off and punishments: and it can't be Christmastime.

"Come on! Everyone back in the car!" and a quarter of an hour later, with the same patent boots and lace-up ankle boots, we were in the Emporium on the hunt for new baubles. Only Delfina's slippers had remained at home: they had to beware not to step on all those shards of coloured glass, while she swept them up.
There wasn't a great deal of choice at the Emporium, everyone knows you shouldn't leave it to the last minute if you want really nice baubles. But our owns, which lived in old wooden wine crates for 350 days a year, had just betrayed us. They had suddenly become a carpet of shiny shards, and after years of distinguished service, they had inexplicably decided they didn't want to stay in our house any longer. And who knows what on earth they had in mind, because we had treated them so well… serves them right! From that year on, the little glass bird had some new neighbours.

Our father was flabbergasted. For generations, he had carefully preserved delicate antique hand-painted glass ornaments, and now, there before him stood a tree full of plastic baubles in pop colours, out of which smiled some Disney comic characters: Mickey Mouse with Minnie on the bottom right, Snow White and the Seven Dwarfs (each one had its own bauble) to the east, Horace, Clarabel, Huey, Dewey and Louie on the top left just above Gus Goose and Gladstone Gander…
"What happened?" he said in a small voice, staring at the resin-perfumed Disneyland before him. It was an aesthetic disaster, and this time he couldn't even blame it on Gambucci.

The lovely thing about Christmas is that, whatever happens, it always remains the same. It's got the strength of time on its side, so even unexpected breaks with tradition never manage to alter its essence. That tree seemed to come from somewhere else, a Martian landed down our chimney like the Befana (and try to imagine the Befana dressed like Twiggy!), but it played its part to the end. It hosted all the parcels beneath its branches, it shone brightly in the night beside the fireplace, and even if it had a huge red grosgrain bow on the top instead of the star, the little glass bird was more than happy. He had chosen a sheltered branch (with children nearby who knows what might happen…) and stayed there until Epiphany. I couldn't say that his livery of feathers sprayed with gold made much of an impression, in the midst of all those brash colours: it looked like Great Aunt Gaetana at a Beatles concert, but for us he was still beautiful… much like tidy square hedges were for Gambucci.

I always think of this story, every time I bring the little glass bird out of his box at Christmas. He's become a little less shy, over the years, he goes around the house hopping here and there. He has a spring on his leg that comes off, a hole in one wing, and sometimes he forgets his tail of nylon bristles, but do you know anyone who doesn't get an ailment as they get older? I continue to keep him with me, from house to house, from year to year, because without him it wouldn't be Christmas. What's more, I think he is still beautiful…

stories

Orange jelly – or lemon if you prefer

If you can make fresh juice or cut an apple into quarters, you can also make this jelly. As it doesn't contain pectin, it relies solely on the natural pectin content of the apples. The only job you need to do is to find unwaxed fruit (you need to use the apple skin and lemon zest) and a very fine iron sieve, which will be very useful for a lot of other things. This is a basic level recipe, so go for it! Even if you never thought you could make your own jam. With the following quantities, you'll make enough for at least two jars. You could keep one for yourself (orange jelly is delicious on a slice of toasted black bread with salted butter, or in a fruit tart) and give the other to a dear friend. If your friend adores black bread, you could also give him or her a nice loaf of sapa bread (recipe on p. 23). It lasts a long time and is perfect for these jellies.

TIME: 1½ HOURS

MAKES TWO 300 ML/10 FL OZ JARS

ORANGE JELLY

750-800 g/just over 1 ½ lb unwaxed
    apples (not too mature)
1 kg/2.2 lb unwaxed blood oranges
½ unwaxed lemon
About 500 g/1.1 lb caster sugar

LEMON JELLY

750-800 g/just over 1 ½ lb unwaxed
    apples (not too mature)
600-700 g/1.3-1 ½ lb unwaxed
    lemons
About 500 g/1.1 lb caster sugar

1. Wash the apples well. Cut them into large pieces (I make 4 quarters then divide each one into 2) without peeling or removing the seeds or core.

2. Put them in a high-sided iron pan and cover with cold water (just under the surface of the apples). It doesn't matter if your pan is wide or narrow; it is important that the apples are compact and not bobbing about all over the place. The water level should be about a centimetre/0.3" below the surface of the fruit. Cook uncovered over a medium heat for about 30 minutes. The apples should be tender but not mushy (if they are soft to the touch of a fork, they're ready).

3. Now drain them and collect all the juice. The operation is very simple but you need to be careful regarding various aspects, so here are the details:
A couple of tips. Number one: the apple juice is the pectin that will thicken your jelly, so you mustn't waste a drop…
Number two: the amount of apple juice you can collect will dictate how much jelly you will get. To give you some idea, 30 ml/1 fl oz of juice less at this stage means about 90 ml/3 fl oz less jelly at the end. Do you feel like renouncing?
Now you've got the idea: don't lose even a drop of juice!
Drain the apples with the help of a fine sieve. It's a good idea to collect the liquid straight into a graduated jug, then place the sieve over a bowl. Delicately pressing on the apples with a spoon, extract as much juice as you can. It'll probably take about ten minutes, but it's worth it. Be gentle (the apple pulp mustn't get through the sieve or it will make your jelly cloudy) but firm; keep the sieve slightly tilted and continue to press, even if only a few drops come out at a time. You should manage to collect about 250 ml/8.4 fl oz, with patience.

4. Now squeeze the oranges, filter the juice (with the help of a teaspoon) and measure it according to the amount of apple juice you have. To clarify: if you have 250 ml/8.4 fl oz apple juice, you'll need 250 ml/8.4 fl oz orange juice (if you have a little less or a little more, adjust the quantity of orange juice).

recipes

5. Peel the zest from the lemon half with a small sharp knife (including the white part) and squeeze as much juice as you can. Filter it and add to the orange and apple juices, with a couple of seeds that you can easily remove after cooking.

6. Now measure all the juices together and weigh the equivalent amount of sugar. Let's suppose you have 250 ml/8.4 fl oz apple juice, you'll have 250 ml/8.4 fl oz orange juice plus 30 ml/1 fl oz lemon juice: so you'll need 530 g/1.1 lb sugar.

7. Put the juices and the sugar in the pan that you have already used to cook the apples (without washing it); mix to allow the sugar to dissolve and then switch on the heat. Cook over a high heat for 10-15 minutes from boiling point. Mix from time to time and remove the foam that forms on the surface. After the first 10 minutes, test the consistency of the jelly by putting a teaspoonful on a cold plate that has been in the freezer. Within a few seconds, it should become dense but not solid (bearing in mind that it will continue to coagulate a little once cool).

8. Pour into a jam jar while it is still boiling hot and let cool before putting the lid on (or covering with cling film). It will keep in the fridge for at least 2 months.

For the lemon jelly

Follow the recipe for orange jelly through all its stages, substituting the oranges for lemons.

Miss out stage 5; just add the zest and seeds of 1 lemon with the apple and lemon juices before putting them in the pan with the sugar.

Christmas is a wreath,
*a snowflake,
hundreds of tiny lights*

Sugar *snowflakes*

You will need:
2 egg whites, 400 g/14 oz fine caster sugar, icing sugar, a piping bag with a small nozzle, parchment paper, sellotape

1. Draw some snowflakes on some white paper and anchor the paper to the worktop with sellotape. Prepare a large piece of parchment paper.

2. Whip the egg whites, adding the sugar gradually; use an electric whisk because the mixture is very heavy.

3. When the mixture becomes shiny and puffs up, put it into the piping bag and use for tracing over the snowflakes on the parchment paper (hold the paper down with weights, and move it along a little after every flake). Work quickly as it dries fast.

4. Let your work of art have its own snowfall of icing sugar and leave to dry for 24 hours. The flakes are fragile but edible: don't tell the foodies in your house or you'll be left with nothing but crumbs!

A garland of stars

YOU'LL NEED:

citrus and pomegranate skins, small biscuit cutters, a large needle, thin string

1. Peel the citrus fruits and the pomegranate with a sharp knife.
2. Cut out stars with your metal biscuit cutters (you'll need to press hard: work on a chopping board if you want to avoid turning your best table into a starry sky…).
3. Make a hole in each one with a large wool needle or a kilt pin, thread them onto a small knitting needle and leave to dry for at least a day.
4. Thread the string along the needle and make your garland. If a star breaks, pop it into the jar of pot-pourri (on the next page). If someone in your family isn't too keen on eating fruit, seize the moment to convince them; the rule is that you can only cut out the skin of the fruit they have eaten themselves…

Pot-pourri
in a pan

You'll need:
apples, pears, fresh ginger, citrus skins, cinnamon sticks, cloves, star anise, peppercorns, juniper berries

1. Thinly slice the apples, pears and ginger, and the citrus skins into little stars. Dry in the oven at 100°C/210°F (they shouldn't darken, so keep an eye on them).

2. Leave to dry completely for a day or two (there should be no trace of dampness), and then put everything into glass jars with the spices.

3. Simmer a good handful of pot-pourri every time you fancy (or you feel the need) for the aroma of Christmas.

String lanterns

You'll need:
balloons, heavy string, PVA glue, a flat paintbrush

1. Blow up the balloons, wrap string around them, slightly overlapping, and then paint plenty of glue over the entire surface. Hang them with clothes pegs and leave to dry for a few hours.

2. When the string is hard, pop the balloons and remove all the residues.

3. The balls are beautiful if you fill them with tiny lights. Use the type of lights that don't heat up. You can forget the idea of using candles if you would rather not spend Christmas night with the fire brigade…

Christmas is a gift...

It wouldn't be Christmas without presents. Do you know anyone who would disagree? I'd like to tell you what a Christmas gift means to me, what it has that is special or different, and why I couldn't ever give up those hours spent among wrapping paper, ribbons, glue, jars and boxes… or afternoons in the kitchen, if possible in the company of helpers as excited as me about the idea of competing with professionals such as Father Christmas or the Befana (this would be impossible, given their years of experience, but we should always follow a "high" example).

Irrespective of its contents, value and the person on the receiving end, a Christmas gift means a beautiful parcel. Even the smallest thought becomes a gift if we wrap it carefully; it's a way of saying: "I've thought of you, I've dedicated time to you and I want you to really enjoy unwrapping this…". Whether you keep the parcels under the tree, in a row above the fireplace, or in a basket by the sofa, lovely parcels contribute greatly to creating a real atmosphere. In this sense, they become a gift for you, too, until the recipients open them! So don't limit yourself to buying: it's not enough at Christmastime.

Wrapping paper

Choose the same paper for everyone (or coordinating paper) and transform the parcels into part of your home decor. If the boutique bag disappears inside its chosen wrapping, all the better; it'll be a great surprise once opened! Here is a couple of ideas that we all love in our house (which we enjoy changing from year to year):

• Varese paper (the type once used to line drawers, with small designs) are beautiful; I always keep a good supply. You can try wrapping with different colours using contrasting ribbons (red designs with green ribbon and vice versa, for example), to separate gifts for boys and girls (without an age limit), or for grown-ups and children. You could choose a range of designs of the same colour;

• heavy parcel paper, which costs a lot less than wrapping paper and can be made to look very elegant, is an alternative with many advantages. As it comes in brown or white (leave the opaque side outwards), you can choose beautiful ribbons (velvet, grosgrain and simple string all work well), along with something special from your garden. If someone in your family writes lovely calligraphy, ask them to write the name of the recipient with a felt tip pen – in a repeating pattern, as a motif – before proceeding to the wrapping. If no-one possesses this skill, you can use rubber stamps. If you have small paper cutters (mini hole punches, I believe they are called), with Christmas shapes, cut out stars, trees and suchlike to stick on your parcels with a drop of glue (children love doing this job).

Ribbons, tags and decorations

I never understood the beauty of so-called "gift ribbons", the type that curls up easily. If you think like me, you'll know that cotton ribbon (which you can buy in a haberdasher's and costs the same as gift ribbon) will guarantee a much more stunning effect and they curl just as easily, too; no cascading ringlets, mind you…

Cord and string of varying sizes and colours (bicoloured cotton and kitchen string) work well, too. Their simple appearance means you can choose beautiful accessories such as pine cones, berries, holly twigs, orange or pomegranate-skin stars (from the garland on p. 178), cinnamon sticks, star anise, little bells (jingle bells!), the biscuits on p. 35 and the crackers on p. 62 (crunch! crunch!)… well, you're spoilt for choice! Regarding edible decorations, just make sure your foodies (of the two or four-legged varieties) keep their distance until the night of the 25th.

Finally, gift tags. A parcel without a gift tag is a gift without heart, and you'd need some courage to give presents without heart at Christmas…so be prepared. If you use those with an envelope, find an affectionate phrase suitable for each person (make an effort; even the sourest of elderly aunts has the right to receive heart-warming wishes at Christmas). Otherwise you could opt for parcel labels, which you can personalise with the name of the recipient and a small picture. A fun alternative, if you can find them, is to use self-adhesive old-fashioned luggage labels, oval or square and rather retro.

With love, from me to you...

Christmas is a sense of expectation... naturally, this also applies to presents! Those to be received, but also those to make, if you wish to make them yourself. There are so many possibilities among these pages but here are some ideas, in order of appearance:

All the biscuits of the chapter "The biscuit tin" can be made in advance and they'll keep well in a tin. If the recipient is someone who loves cooking, the biscuits made with spices and cocoa (p. 35) can be transformed into a kit. Mix all the dry ingredients and put them in a hermetically sealed jar; top it with a suitable biscuit cutter and attach a lovely label with the instructions (it couldn't be more simple: they just have to pour the contents of the jar into a mixer with a few other ingredients).
If you like the idea of a "jar-biscuit-cutter-instructions" kit, you can do the same thing with the seeded rye crackers (p. 62), which also offer you the opportunity to add a good cheese or a bottle of wine to go with them, creating a nice aperitif. If you'd like to make another kit, use the *pain d'épices* recipe (p. 27); a jar of delicious honey would go perfectly with it.

If, however, you prefer a wreath, you can make the meringue (p. 131), or the cracker version (p. 61, which can be accompanied by a box of camembert of a suitable size). You can prepare both these wreaths well in advance, but be very careful when transporting. If your gift also contains a nice serving dish or a wooden cheese board, the recipient can use their gift straightaway.

For lovers of bingo, board games, and all those convivial situations in which a delicious nibble or two is much appreciated, the recipes from the chapter "The bingo table" will be perfect. Mini cake cases and boxes are ideal for toffee and chocolate truffles, as well as the sesame crunch, which, like its almond cousin, can be gifted whole, with or without a Christmas shape. As far as nougat (p. 56) is concerned, you might like to gift it whole, too, with its chocolate coating, or cut it into squares and dip them in chocolate, drying them well before putting it into a box (you'll create the most delicious mini-nougats).

Foodies will also love receiving nuts in honey and salt. As they are so quick to prepare, be generous: three different jars – hazelnuts, almonds and cashews – to suit all tastes (p. 72).
If you like the idea of sets of jars, you have at least two alternative options: a sweet one, with a trio of syrups (pomegranate, pear and ginger, and mulled wine, p. 162 and 165), and one sweet/savoury with a fun exotic touch: chutney parade (p. 76-78)! Both solutions allow you to prepare well in advance.

For the liver and port pâté (p. 68), one solitary jar will suffice... it will be good even if you don't get your livers from Signor Vittorio, but as it doesn't keep for long, you can prepare it a couple of days at most in advance. In case you want to present it at one of those "bring a contribution" buffets, organise yourself before and arrive at your friends' house with a loaf of sapa bread (p. 23): sliced and toasted, it makes the perfect companion for the pâté (you could also add a bottle of Sauternes to complete your gift, but this is optional). If you happen to remember the party at the last minute, put together a couple of cold salads: the cucumber salad, and the marinated apples and herrings (p. 119 and 120 respectively) can be prepared in a few minutes. They are unusual but Christmassy and will be a welcome addition to any buffet. Something else that is essential to any gathering of friends at Christmas is a light hint of alcohol, like the syrup for mulled wine (p. 165) or Hypocras (p. 158), quite innocuous.
Finally, for a little tradition: two citrus jellies (p. 172 and 173), delicious, clear and beautiful, perfect to give to a friend who always asks where you got those little jars (so make sure the jars you use are exactly the ones she loves).

Now to Granny, the romantic of the family who believes that Christmas isn't Christmas without snow, and that the seasons aren't like they used to be, in her day there was a lot more snow. Make an effort and prepare the most beautiful snowfall she will ever seen: sugar snowflakes (p. 177) and... let there be Christmas!

When using yeast
Some useful tips for those who haven't used yeast before

1. Liquid temperatures

Yeast usually needs to "reawaken" by dissolving in a liquid, often with other ingredients. Whether its morning bath happens alone or in company, the temperature should never be above that gentle warmth that allows it to carry out its task without *défaillances*. Cold will hold it back, excessive heat will kill it, so the best thing you can do is to consider its temperature equal to human body temperature. Dip a finger into the liquid and if you can't tell the difference, it'll be just right. Always check that the small pan you have warmed up is not too hot (the yeast won't like it). If you have a graduated jug, transfer everything into it (liquid, yeast, and all the ingredients that go with it in this initial stage): its temperature will be fine and you can check when the contents have doubled in volume by checking the quantity markings.

2. A warm place...

When you see "a warm place" written in the recipe, this doesn't mean an oven which has just been switched off, or Grandpa's chair by the fireplace, or a radiator. Yeast in the process of working will be fine in a corner of your worktop (uncovered, if you've just dissolved the yeast in the liquid, or covered if it has already been mixed into a dough), just make sure it won't be subjected to brusque temperature variations. If you have to throw open the windows because you've burnt the roast, and outside there's a storm raging, park it in another room. Don't forget about it, though; it's more than capable of coming out of the jug (or bowl) to come and find you...

3. How to make dough by hand

Making a dough by hand is much easier than you think, and allows you to control the fruits of your labours "hands on". I use two techniques, one for a firm dough and one for the sticky variety; you can even alternate the techniques during the same recipe, depending on the situation.

Firm doughs: "snakes and snails" is a sequence of twisting between 10-12 times, for a total of 10 minutes working time.

1. Roll the dough beneath your hands until you have a snake of about 60 cm/23", more or less.
2. Turn it 90°, placing it vertically in front of you.
3. Roll it up on itself as if it were a snail; keep the outside part nearest to you while the other part is rolled, squashed and lengthened outwards.
4. When you have finished twisting, you'll find the dough in the right position for the next stage.

Sticky doughs: "grab-beat-fold" is a sequence of between 100-200 folds, (don't be put off by the numbers as you'll be able to do this in less than a quarter of an hour), during which you must constantly butter your hands as well as the worktop (this is the best way to incorporate butter into the dough). Remember, though: no flour! Only butter, every time the dough becomes unmanageable...

1. Butter your hands and your worktop.
2. Grab the dough with one hand (or two if the dough is very sticky), lift it and beat it on the worktop without letting it go, letting it lengthen in front of you (you almost have to fan it, as if you're shaking out a tablecloth).
3. Once it has landed, fold it back over onto itself, keeping hold of it all the time.
4. Turn it 90° and repeat the sequence.

Have faith; the dough becomes less sticky as you proceed. If you find you can't get it quite right, leave it for 5-10 minutes beneath an upturned bowl and then start again where you left off.

4. The rising room

The best environment, in terms of temperature and humidity, you can create at home that is ideal for allowing a prepared dough mixture to rise, is in the form of a plastic bag; if possible one that you use for (don't laugh) keeping clothes in when you make the seasonal wardrobe changeover. When you read: "a large, well-sealed, inflated plastic bag..." in the recipes, you need to imagine one of those plastic bags for jackets (the perfect size) placed on my kitchen table, tightly knotted at the end where a hanger would go, and more loosely tied at the other end (as I have to reopen that one). Inside the bubble (the bag needs to be inflated so that it doesn't stick to its precious content), the dough will rise calmly in its mould or in its baking tray, allowing me to check its progress. The bag can be re-used, but perfumes are banned: so no lavender, Oriental nights or Ocean breeze – they harm both moths and brioches.

Index

Index of stories

Acknowledgements

I would not have been able to complete this project without the encouragement and affection of the readers of "Fragole a Merenda". As I didn't write a post on the blog for months, they went looking for me: lovely e-mails, gifts, thoughts full of friendship and words that I will never forget. They were my source of energy when my reserves were low, and, once again, my initial thanks go to them.

Thank you to Alessandra Costa, without whom the idea of a Christmas book would never have entered my head. It seemed to me a fabulous idea and… irresistible! I have much appreciated her advice and invaluable support: this book owes a lot to her, and I also owe her the discovery of a restaurant that I have not stopped visiting since.

Thank you to Guido Tommasi who continues to be the editor of my favourite cookbooks, independent of the fact that he now publishes my own, too. Once again, I was granted the rare privilege of following my work at every stage: I know it's unusual for an author, and I am extremely grateful for that.

Thank you to Anita Ravasio, who has skilfully steered this ship into port, using creative manoeuvres which only the most expert captains can carry out, and calmly put up with my inability to understand her foliation calculation sheets (close relatives of Google algorithm, I assure you).

Thank you to Carolina Quaresima, who created the layout with great enthusiasm, and to Anna Pecchio and Giusy Marzano, who reread with patience and great respect my texts.

And now a few thanks of a different kind, because this is a book that goes deep into the recesses of my affections and my past. My first thought is for my grandparents: every Christmas memory is associated with their great big house, and the preparations for our Christmas lunch (they went on for days!). And if I hadn't had 21 cousins (yes, 21…) on hand to try everything, my cake-making experiments would not have gone beyond the odd timid attempt.

Thank you to my parents for the wonderful Christmases of my childhood, and to my brother and sister who were very much an integral part of those Christmases (and not just in photographs).

Thank you to my children, who accepted to have Sunday lunch at the Indian curry house round the corner for an entire winter, because our dining room table resembled Father Christmas's desk. Principessa's friends contributed, hoovering up any kind of Christmas edible with no sign of flagging, even at the beginning of the warm season. As for her brother, certain jokes he made have entered our family annals for good ("Is that Tolstoy's house? Has Signora finished, or is she still writing 'War and Peace'?").

Now to Polpetta, who wrote a couple of chapters with me in a four-handed keyboard duet: well, if the truth be known, she cancelled them, pressing down on the keys in the hope that our favourite video of "The Jungle Book" would appear, so I had to write them again... and then we'd start dancing around together like Mowgli and Baloo.

Thank you to that terribly serious gentleman, who – in one of life's unexpected little ironies – became first Monsieur d'Aubergine and then incredibly funny. I owe my survival during the months of writing this book to him and his evening culinary performances: his "vermicelli cacio e pepe" is now unrivalled, so much so that no-one laughs anymore when he messes about in the kitchen with the air of a witch doctor. As I sent him to buy so many spices for me, he's also made friends with the grocer: to avoid any questions as to what he does with all that star anise, cardamom and cinnamon, he asks him to recommend some excellent wines. So we always begin our dinner by proposing a toast: "To us and to life!".

Well, we've come to talk about life at the end, almost without meaning to, but at just the right moment. Thank you to life itself, that extraordinary adventure which continues to amaze me, one little scene at a time, day by day. I find it fantastic, and not just at Christmas. And I believe I will never stop loving it…

© Guido Tommasi Editore – Datanova S.r.l., 2018

Text and photographs: Sabrine d'Aubergine
Graphics: Carolina Quaresima
Editing: Anita Ravasio

Any reproduction, partial or total, on any device,
in particular photocopy and microfilm, is strictly prohibited
without the express written permission of the publisher.

ISBN: 978 88 6753 245 2

Printed in Italy